FIRST STEP INTO
BHAGAVAD GITA

Essential Groundwork to Comprehend the Human Crisis

GITA ODYSSEY SERIES: 1

RAJESH RABINDRANATH,
DR. VIKRANT SINGH TOMAR,
AVANTI KUNDALIA

INDIA • SINGAPORE • MALAYSIA

ISBN 979-8-89186-780-2

Table of Contents

About the Authors

Avanti Kundalia

Avanti Kundalia is a Vedanta teacher and life coach based in Singapore. Through ongoing intensive research and rigorous experimentation, she has dedicated her life to validating the efficacy of Vedantic teachings in daily life. A mother of two, Avanti finds her greatest fulfillment in teaching the Bhagavad Gita to all age groups in relatable ways that guarantee dramatic inner transformations. Her insightful writings on Vedanta and beautiful translations of spiritual texts in English are well-loved by seekers of truth. A true patriot of Bharat, Avanti has been championing the cause of Sanatan Dharma traditions across the globe, especially with householders.

Rajesh Rabindranath

Rajesh Rabindranath is a multifaceted technology and management professional who harmonizes his engagement with modern innovations, particularly artificial intelligence, with a passion for Vedantic teachings. Based in New Jersey, USA, he passionately imparts the timeless wisdom of the Bhagavad Gita through regular classes and at diverse forums, including corporate events and interfaith gatherings. As a co-founder and devoted volunteer of the nonprofit organization Project Self, Rajesh is deeply committed to spreading spiritual awareness. Rajesh's personal life reflects the harmonious blend of worldly responsibilities and spiritual pursuits, as he finds joy in moments spent with his wife, Deepthy, and daughter, Daksha.

Dr. Vikrant Singh Tomar

Dr. Vikrant Singh Tomar is a globally acknowledged scholar, writer, and management consultant. He is nominated by Civil 20 (under G-20) as the 'International Coordinator,' for the "Vasudhaiva Kutumbakam", to promote in G-20 Nations. He addressed the United Nations Headquarters in Geneva on the International Day of Conscience. He is the global convener of the World Yoga Summit in Germany in 2023. He is also nominated by the Indian Council of Cultural Relations as the 'International Coordinator' for the Global Conference on Holistic Yoga Beyond Physiology 2023 in Germany. He is the Director of Project Inc. USA, Convenor of 'United Consciousness Global', and Board Member of the European Yoga Federation and Spiritual Council in Africa. He is also the Honorary Dean of SVYASA University, Bangalore.

Forward from Respected Dr. H.R. Nagendra

Bangalore,
November 14th, 2023

While there have been many books on the Bhagavadgita over decades, if not centuries, by renowned authors, updated versions continue to pour in, bringing newer and relevant dimensions to this great text. Among the triplet of our spiritual heritage consisting of Shruti (Upanishads), Smrti (edited texts of the Upanishads such as the Bhagavad Gita), and Nyaaya (Brahma Sutras) Prasthana, the Bhagavadgita provides the sum and substance of the entire knowledge base of our creation and beyond as found in the Upanishads.

Modern science over the last 400 years has fathomed the structure (energy at the base of all matter) and laws (classical and Quantum mechanics) of the physical world and is moving further to understand the subtler and causal dimensions of the entire creation. The Upanishads unraveled the whole creation, consisting of five layers of the universe (known as Pancha Koshas – *Annamaya, Pranamaya, Manomaya, Vijnanamaya, and Anandamaya Koshas*), which continuously change, governed by the triplet law of Creation, Sustenance, and Destruction, made out of *Chitta* (mind) and that which is beyond and does not change, called as Brahman or Reality. To bring this total knowledge base, the Gita systematically presents it in its 700 slokas across 18 chapters, with each chapter called a Yoga and representing the most comprehensive text on Yoga.

"First Step into Bhagavad Gita" is the inaugural volume of the Gita Odyssey series, an ambitious project by Project Self, aiming to bridge the ancient wisdom of the Bhagavad Gita with contemporary intellect. This book is an invitation to embark on a transformative journey through the enlightening insights of the Gita, a scripture that stands as a timeless voice of wisdom, resonating across ages with humanity's heart.

The book is designed as an accessible, step-by-step guide through the complexities of human life, making the profound teachings of the Bhagavad Gita relatable to seekers from all walks of life. Reflecting the collective spiritual experiences of its authors - the Author Trio from Project Self, the book is a testament to their desire to connect every heart with the Gita's timeless wisdom.

In essence, this book is more than just a guide to the Gita's teachings; it is a pathway to personal transformation, inviting readers to explore and understand. I am confident that the book will attract a large audience seeking deeper knowledge dimensions contained in the Bhagavadgita. I wish all the best for the success of this first volume brought out by the authors.

Dr H.R. Nagendra
Chancellor, S-VYASA University,
Bangalore, India

Section I

Beginning the Odyssey

"Step into the Gita and discover the essence of life's most profound truths."

Introduction

Project Self welcomes you to embark on a transformative journey through the enlightening insights of the Bhagavad Gita. Amidst the vast expanse of spiritual literature, the Bhagavad Gita echoes as the timeless voice of wisdom, speaking directly to the heart of humanity across all time and space. We are deeply honored to introduce the inaugural volume of the Gita Odyssey series, a collection of 18 books - each meticulously crafted to harmonize ancient wisdom with the modern intellect. Through this monumental endeavor, our humble aspiration is to render the profound teachings of the Bhagavad Gita easily accessible and more relatable to today's seekers. Rooted in the authentic teachings of Advaita Vedanta, we trust that this commentary on the Bhagavad Gita will transcend the realm of intellectual delight. It is designed to be a personally guided, step-by-step expedition through the complexities of human life. This book is intended for individuals from all walks of life who aspire to reach their highest potential, cultivate inner peace and contentment, and strive toward the ultimate goal of Self-Realization. It is crafted for sincere seekers who wish to unearth practical insights buried within the depth of scriptural wisdom and apply them to their daily lives. No prior knowledge of Advaita Vedanta or the Bhagavad Gita is necessary to derive value from this book. All that is required is an open mind and a strong desire for knowledge.

The Heartfelt Journey Behind the Words

This book reflects the collective spiritual experiences and aspirations of all the members of Project Self, particularly those of the author Trio. It stands as a testament to our earnest desire to connect every heart with the timeless wisdom of the Bhagavad Gita.

The Personal Conviction

We passionately believe that the teachings of the Gita, when rightly understood and diligently applied, carry the potential to transform any life. Intensive study of the Bhagavad Gita has reshaped our perceptions and filled our lives with purpose. It is this transformation that we wish to share with the world.

Recognizing the Underutilization

Today, the Bhagavad Gita, despite the reverence it commands, often remains only partially understood by the masses. While many recognize its religious significance, only a few venture deep enough to tap into its transformative power. It is worth noting that this profound scripture is often used only as a source of fleeting solace during challenging times, which is akin to owning a cutting-edge supercomputer but using it merely as a calculator. Recognizing this heavy underutilization of so potent a scriptural text, we committed to this mission of reintroducing a more holistic version of the Gita and highlighting its undisputed relevance for the contemporary mind.

Addressing the Challenges Hindering Study in Modern Times

The sincere seeker of today encounters numerous challenges. Gone are the days of structured Vedic teaching methodologies, and many find themselves adrift in the vast ocean of spirituality. Subtle truths are often lost in translation. Unfamiliarity with the Sanskrit language and conflicting interpretations arising from differing metaphysical standpoints further obstruct spiritual growth. Our goal is to offer a clear, systematic path firmly rooted in the Advaita Vedanta tradition.

Designed for the Contemporary Seeker

The systematic and highly disciplined traditional methods of presenting the Gita may not always resonate with the contemporary mind. Our motivation was also fueled by the desire to translate age-old wisdom into a language and context that speaks directly to the modern discerning intellect, making it relatable and relevant.

For the Householders and Professionals

There is a common belief that the Bhagavad Gita is primarily intended for individuals in the later stages of life or exclusively for renunciates. We have tried to highlight the practicality and relevance of these teachings, especially for householders and professionals, through various angles throughout the book. We, the Author Trio and members of Project Self, though deeply entrenched in our professional and household lives, continue to be guided through every step by the teachings of the Gita. We felt a compelling need, backed by our lived experiences, to assure seekers like us that the Bhagavad Gita proves to be the most useful manual within the everyday life context than out of it.

Giving Back to the Source

We took on the Gita Odyssey production to express our gratitude and pay homage to the scriptures and our revered teachers. Through this series, we aim to convey the sense of purpose and direction gained through our study and application of this life-transforming text. Our aspiration is to bridge generation gaps and make the efficacy of the Gita's timeless wisdom a reality in as many lives as possible.

Structure of this Book

The first of the "Gita Odyssey" series was conceptualized to familiarize you with the foundational knowledge necessary to study the Gita. Our purpose was to lay a firm foundation upon which our collective understanding of these invaluable teachings of the Gita would evolve. To achieve this objective, we have meticulously organized this book into five distinct sections. Each preceding one is a building block for a clearer comprehension of the next section.

Section I: Beginning the Odyssey

In this section, the Author Trio shares their combined vision that initiated this literary journey. A swift dive into their collaborative thought processes, as it were, will help you better connect with the rhythm and flow of the commentary.

Section II: Preparing for the Journey: Essential Knowledge for a Meaningful Study:

In what we consider the most pivotal section of this volume, we have explored the foundational concepts that will provide a solid framework for studying the Bhagavad Gita. This portion will equip you with:

- A comprehension of the essence and significance of the Bhagavad Gita.
- Insights into its relevance, especially in an era dominated by Artificial Intelligence.
- Techniques and approaches for a compelling study.
- A historical perspective of the Gita's origins and evolution.
- An exploration of the common myths and misunderstandings surrounding the Gita and their subsequent debunking.
- An overview of the Gita's profound influence on luminaries worldwide.

Section III: Gita Dhyanam: A Meditative Prelude:

The third section contains a unique exposition of the invocation verses, revered as the Gita Dhyanam, that will render every reader's mind and intellect more receptive to the profound knowledge to follow. A comprehensive introduction and a verse-by-verse analysis of the Gita Dhyanam promises to enrich your understanding and appreciation of these deeply meditative verses.

Section IV: Arjuna Vishada Yoga: What Prompted the Wisdom of the Bhagavad Gita

The worth and value of the first chapter are hugely underrated - and often-overlooked. A thorough understanding of its verses, as attempted in this book, makes it a treasure trove of insights, revealing the unfathomable complicatedness of the human psyche. Though set against a particular backdrop of ancient Indian history, the teachings from this first chapter are undeniably perennial. Our well-articulated commentary correlates the historical battlefield to the realities of mortal struggles by positing the Mahabharata war as an analogy for our equally devastating inner battles.

Section V: Reflections and Forward Glance:

Section V briefly revisits the ground we have covered and introduces you to the "Divine Canvas" project of which this book is a part. The authors individually express their thoughts and feelings about what has been a soul-stirring journey. Such an elaborate prelude to the text has been carefully designed to provide a comprehensive context that will keep you firmly anchored through the meandering conversational flow of the Bhagavad Gita.

Inviting You to the Odyssey

Dear Reader,

We heartily congratulate you for choosing to embark on this transformative journey. Our intent is for you to gain a better understanding of the Bhagavad Gita and, in the process, experience a profound inner transformation. We encourage you to form an intimate bond with this timeless wisdom, which, if rightly imbibed, will see you through all the peaks and valleys of your life.

We recommend you explore this book in its intended sequence. After each section, take a moment to contemplate and assimilate what you have learned. Pose questions to yourself, deliberate over gaps in understanding that may appear, tussle with your curiosities, and allow what you have comprehended to marinate in your mind. Doing so will strengthen your intellectual understanding and help you develop a heartfelt connection with the text.

To further fortify your study, we have developed a complementary e-learning course that mirrors the themes and insights of this book. This course will prove invaluable to reinforce and deepen your comprehension. You can embark on this e-learning expedition by registering at https://Gitaodyssey.org.

Our website will continue to upload additional supplementary materials that will keep you up-to-date and enthusiastically connected with the ever-evolving nature of these teachings.

Our commitment to sharing this wisdom goes beyond the written word. We invite you to join Project Self's vibrant virtual community on our YouTube channel and various social media platforms. You will find many videos, discussions, and insights to fortify your learnings further.

Lastly, we offer live, instructor-led classes on the Bhagavad Gita for those who wish to make the understanding and application of its teachings an ongoing part of their daily spiritual practice or *sadhana*. These interactive classes foster a safe place to engage in elaborate reflections and discussions. We also offer a Bhagavad Gita Teacher Training Course for anyone inspired to share this knowledge with others formally.

Rest assured, you are not alone in your quest; we walk this path with you, hand in hand. We pray our collective learnings help us all emerge transformed.

Yours sincerely,

Avanti Kundalia, Rajesh Rabindranath, and Dr.Vikrant Singh Tomar

Project Self Team

Avneet Baid, Deepthy Nair, Gokul Kallambunathil, Jeena Suresh, Karthik Palamalai, Madhurika Arvind, Muthuvelan Swaminathan, Dr. Prasad Akavoor, Rajesh Menon, Sanjay Rajput, Sunil Veettil, Suresh Kadavath and Dr. Vijay Reddy

Gita Insight Squad

Bhuvana Iyer (Guidance), Ramurti Shrivastava (Poetry), Kavalam Srikumar (Chanting), K.I Alexander (Music), Muktha Sathe (Music), Sreya Sajan (Painting) and Pradeep Krishnan (Malayalam Translation) and Dr. K. Unnikrishnan Namboothiri (Sanskrit)

Sponsors and Supporters

Rohit & Bharati Metha, Kiran Kumar Nair, United Consciousness, Bhakti Manjari Group, and Sadhaka Music Foundation

Cover Painting

Sreya Sajan

Shloka Script Courtesy

Avadhoota Datta Peetham

Preparing for the Journey

Essential Knowledge for Meaningful Study

"Sound preparation smoothens the path of any journey, ensuring each step is taken with purpose and clarity."

Relevance of Bhagavad Gita in Modern Times

We inhabit a world driven by technology. We have indiscriminate access to overwhelming information. Various branches of science offer numerous solutions to our everyday problems. Artificial Intelligence is continually revolutionizing how we navigate through life. In times of such phenomenal advancements, is it worth investing time and energy in studying an ancient scripture dating back thousands of years? What is the relevance of this book in our modern lives? Do the challenges and concerns of our ancestors even remotely resemble the issues we face today? It is vital to question the necessity to engage with this age-old literature in our present circumstances. As a famous Sanskrit saying goes, '*prayojanam anuddiśya na mandopi pravartate,*' which means that even a fool does not undertake an action without a purpose to fulfill.

The Paradox of Material Progress and Happiness

Have you ever paused to ponder? From womb to tomb, we set off on a frantic frenzy accumulating wealth, name, fame, power, pursuing relationships, or achieving good health, hoping any or all of this will bring us happiness. We have greater access to material comforts and the knowledge and means to achieve it all than our predecessors ever had. Yet, despite these nerve-racking pursuits of relentless acquisition and enjoyment, most people grapple with an underlying sense of unease.

Scientific and technological advancements have expanded our understanding of the universe, even about perplexing laws like those governing subatomic particles or galaxies. Medical advances have provided new and improved treatments for many natural yet merciless bodily and mental ailments that incapacitated or claimed lives in the past. We have been blessed, as it were, by the gift of longevity. Even the least affluent enjoy unbelievable luxuries compared to people just a few decades ago. Palaces of the bygone eras lacked the conveniences we now take for granted. Inventions like the television, smartphone, and countless other gadgets make life easier and connect us better with each other.

However, despite these material comforts, most people experience a pervasive sense of dissatisfaction. Studies and research findings confirm this observation. The World Happiness Report 2021 [1] revealed a global decline in happiness levels for the fourth consecutive year, accompanied by a rise in mental health issues. According to a study published in the journal [2] "Social Psychological and Personality Science," happiness levels in the United States have remained stagnant since the 1970s despite increased wealth and possessions. The economic cost of mental health disorders like depression and anxiety exceeds $1 trillion (about $3,100 per person in the US) annually, as research [3] from the University of Warwick indicates. The American Psychological Association reports [4] a striking increase in stress levels due to work, financial pressures, and societal issues. Additionally, excessive use of social media has been linked to decreased well-being, feelings of loneliness, and depression, as stated in a study [5] published in "Nature Human Behavior."

These observations and statistics underscore the predicament faced by the modern world. Despite unprecedented material progress, humanity has yet to discover true happiness. They emphasize the fact that the pursuit of external achievements alone does not guarantee lasting fulfillment. Although the modern lifestyle, characterized by an active, harried, and fast-paced rhythm, promises material progress, it irrefutably burdens us with stress and anxiety. On the other hand, a passive and less demanding existence, reminiscent of bygone eras, may be devoid of tension and anxiety but fails to provide the necessary material progress—truly the hallmark of a human experience. The question arises: Is it possible to balance the honors of a hardworking life with the basic human need for peace and contentment?

The Transformative Wisdom of the Bhagavad Gita

The answer to this question can be found in the perennial teachings of the Bhagavad Gita. The Gita redirects our habitual extroverted focus toward inner mastery and lasting happiness. We begin to recognize the underlying cause of the bewildering decrease in our contentment despite material progress.

The Bhagavad Gita proposes a unique approach to life that goes beyond linking happiness to conventional notions of achievement. It teaches us that authentic happiness is a state of mind we must cultivate from within. A famous quote by German philosopher Arthur Schopenhauer says [6]: "It is difficult to find happiness within oneself, but it is impossible to find it anywhere else." Think! How foolish it is to seek permanent happiness from an impermanent world?

The Gita presents a holistic vision of life that promises the unfoldment of our highest potential in the material world while ensuring continual spiritual progress. Experiencing both together rewards us with that elusive, lasting peace we all chase and seldom find. The Gita proffers a comprehensive lifestyle program that empowers us to develop self-awareness, gain command over our mental activities, embody noble virtues, enhance efficiency in our actions, heal unresolved emotions, rise above frustrations, foster harmonious relationships with others, develop strength of character, and find freedom from all forms of suffering. This unique vision of the Gita reconciles the secular pursuits of modern times with the spiritual wisdom of ancient traditions.

The Bhagavad Gita invites us to explore the depths of our consciousness. In doing so, we slowly recognize that the creative, sustaining, and even destructive power of the universe lies within our core. This power, as the Gita reveals, is the same in all, being the fundamental force that unifies the entire cosmos despite its glaring diversity. By awakening to this newly discovered spiritual reality, we gradually refine our perception of the world, dissolve our sense of separation, and discover authentic happiness that does not depend on external circumstances.

The Bhagavad Gita also provides practical guidance on navigating the complexities of modern life without compromising our inner peace and happiness. It offers time-tested principles that help us establish healthy boundaries and make conscious choices, especially in the digital age, thus equipping us with the necessary tools and insights to lead a balanced, meaningful, and joyous life.

Now, modern positive psychology also affirms [7] that happiness is not a fleeting occurrence based on luck, nor is it subject to the dictates of external events. It originates from how we interpret and respond to these occurrences. It is a perpetual state of mind that anyone can cultivate through conscious effort. The key is to master our inner world by gaining control over the mind. When we learn to manage our thoughts, emotions, reactions, and responses, we become empowered to determine the quality of our lives.

Ever-constantly directing our efforts toward creating a balance between our inner and outer worlds, we can better navigate the challenges of the modern world. We untether ourselves from societal constraints by liberating ourselves from anxieties and fears. Even the slightest exertion in this direction can enrich our life, making it a more enjoyable, meaningful, and fulfilling experience.

> *"True fulfillment lies not in the abundance of material possessions, but in creating harmony between outer achievements and inner contentment."*

What is the Bhagavad Gita?

What does the word *Bhagavad Gita* mean? What is the subject matter of the Bhagavad Gita? By exploring these questions, to begin with, we gain the clarity to seamlessly investigate the sacred wisdom embedded within this scriptural masterpiece.

The Literal Meaning of the Bhagavad Gita

Sanskrit, an exquisite language, has a unique way of capturing the essence of words. *Gita* translates as 'song,' while *Bhagavad* serves as an adjective for *Gita*, denoting belongingness or association with *Bhagavan*, the Supreme Being endowed with extraordinary qualities. In this light, *Bhagavad Gita* can be understood as 'the song of *Bhagavan*' or 'a song about *Bhagavan*.'

While there are countless songs in the universe, the Bhagavad Gita is unique because it is a song of or about the Divine Essence. It is a celestial melody that carries life-defining wisdom and guidance to benefit every mortal journey.

But who or what is *Bhagavan*? [8] According to the Vishnu Purana, an ancient scripture, 'One who is endowed with *Bhaga* is *Bhagavan*.' *Bhaga* refers to six-fold virtues in infinite measure: knowledge (*Jnana*), dispassion (*Vairagya*), capacity to create, maintain, and resolve (*Virya*), fame (*Yasas*), wealth (*Sri*), and control (*Aisvarya*). Anyone who possesses these virtues in their entirety is *Bhagavan*. *Bhagavan* represents absolute wealth, strength, beauty, knowledge, and renunciation. It is the embodiment of universal principles and cosmic order—the force that governs and controls the intricate workings of the universe. The *Vishnu Purana* also offers another intriguing definition: '*He who understands the creation and dissolution, the appearance and disappearance of beings, wisdom, and ignorance, should be called Bhagavan.*' [8]

The literal meaning of 'Bhagavad Gita' thus unveils itself as a divine song gifted to humanity by Universal Intelligence. A song that helps us live in harmony with the universal laws and principles that govern our existence.

The Subject Matter of the Bhagavad Gita:

The *Bhagavad Gita* serves as a comprehensive life manual for all humanity. It revolves around two central themes: *Brahma Vidya*, the knowledge of the 'Supreme Truth,' and *Yoga Shastra*, a detailed course for the mind and Self-Realization.

Brahma Vidya, or "Knowledge of the Ultimate Truth," talks about the oneness of our own True Identity with the Ultimate Truth - *Brahman*. This knowledge not only reveals the essence of *Brahman* but also introduces us to the nature of the Universal intelligence (*Ishvara*), the universe (*Jagat*), and the individual (*Jiva*). It elucidates their interconnectedness by revealing the common thread that binds them. *Brahma Vidya* answers the question: are *Ishvara*, *Jagat*, and *Jeeva* separate entities or manifestations of a unified Reality? *Brahma Vidya* proffers the most in-depth understanding of 'what is' and makes us aware of the one unifying Reality that forms the substratum of the diversity seen within existence.

Simultaneously, *Yoga Shastra* offers a systematic approach to cultivating a pure, calm, focused, and controlled mind—a prerequisite for material prosperity and the realization of the Self. It gives us the rationale, tools, techniques, and a step-by-step program to develop an optimal state of holistic well-being. Through *Yoga Shastra*, we learn to harness the power of the mind, cultivate emotional balance, and expand our consciousness. These time-tested methods assuredly lead to material abundance and spiritual growth.

The knowledge of the Gita helps thoroughly meld the physical, mental, intellectual, and spiritual dimensions of our being. The invaluable insights and practical guidance of the Gita can be applied to every aspect of our lives. The Bhagavad Gita stands as a timeless testament to the potential within each one of us to awaken to our highest human possibilities and realize the ultimate truth of our existence.

"The Bhagavad Gita – a symphony orchestrated by the Divine guides us toward a purposeful life sustained in pure elation."

***Dharma*: The Essence of the Bhagavad Gita**

The Bhagavad Gita is a limitless reservoir of profound spiritual knowledge gifted to humanity by *Bhagavan*. Its essence can be gleaned in the opening and closing words of this revered scripture.

The first and last words of the Gita are *Dharma* and *Mama*, respectively. When you flip these words, you get *mama dharma*, which means "my *dharma*." Thus, the primary teaching of the Bhagavad Gita is knowing and living by our individual and collective *Dharma*. [9]

But to do so, we first need to understand *Dharma* [10]. *Dharma* is impossible to translate into English as its meaning varies with context. Depending on the context, it can mean anything from conduct, duty, charity, right, justice, virtue, morality, religion, religious merit, to the path of good, works aligned with righteousness. While these meanings are all correct as per their specific contexts, they do not do full justice to the profundity of the Sanskrit word *Dharma* when portrayed as the essence of the Gita.

In and through the investigation of the deeper meaning of *Dharma*, we are transported, as it were, into the very fabric of existence. The word

Dharma, derived from the Sanskrit root "*dhri*," introduces a staggering concept: that which holds everything together, the laws that bring order to a universe that would otherwise descend into chaos. It represents the innate behavior, duty, ethics, virtue, and universal principles that maintain stability and harmony within the overwhelming complexity of the universe.

Dharma, in its essence, is the manifestation of the underlying order and harmony that permeates every aspect of existence. The force that ensures balance and coherence, the very thread that weaves together the intricate web of life. But what upholds this order? What enforces and governs the laws that sustain stability and harmony? *Bhagavan*—Universal Intelligence, the Supreme Being—who oversees and holds the laws of *Dharma* in impeccable balance.

When we closely observe the world around us, we can discern this complex web of perfect order guided by the all-pervading presence of *Bhagavan*. From the smallest subatomic particles to the vast expanse of galaxies, the laws of nature consolidated by *Bhagavan* flawlessly synchronize one aspect of the universe with another. Consider the ceaseless dance of subatomic particles, the stable formation of atoms, or the graceful ballet of celestial bodies in motion and their congruous orbits. It is *Bhagavan* who maintains this composite equilibrium, ensuring that the laws of *Dharma* are upheld in every domain of existence.

This divine order extends far beyond the celestial realm and interpenetrates every aspect of our mortal experience. This enigmatic order is witnessed even within the human body, the most incredible bio-chemical machine known to us. The sophistication of the brain, the rhythmic beating of the heart, and the countless cells and bacteria that coexist within us—all adhere to a set of principles and cohesively function together, maintaining a perfect balance. Medical science continues to decipher this inherent order, an incalculable expression of *Bhagavan*'s wisdom.

Dharma manifests in various forms: physical *Dharma*, which governs the stability and harmony of the physical universe; body *Dharma*, which ensures the well-being and balance of our bodies; and social *Dharma*, which upholds the strength and unity of society.

What exactly is a dharmic life if *Dharma* is understood as a collection of laws facilitating stability and harmony? A dharmic person adopts a lifestyle that uncompromisingly conforms to *Dharma* and is attuned to the guidance of *Bhagavan*. Such alignment is crucial in ensuring stability and harmony in our lives and society.

Any violation of *Dharma* disrupts this perfect equilibrium overseen by *Bhagavan*. For example, disregarding traffic rules puts all the order of the roads into disarray, causing non-negotiable jams or, worse still, accidents. Neglecting a healthy lifestyle disturbs the balance of our bodies, and violating the laws of nature and ecology jeopardizes environmental stability (think of the consequences of global warming). When we rub against the order of *Dharma*, it rubs back harder, inflicting pain and suffering—a gentle reminder from *Bhagavan*, as it were, to realign with the cosmic order. [10]

The ancient sages, in all their wisdom, implore us through their teachings to imbibe dharmic values, for they award us a life of harmony where our actions and choices resonate with the pulse of creation itself. In doing so, we commit to aligning with the universal laws that govern our existence.

Everyone has a unique *Dharma*, a calling that resonates with their inherent nature and core purpose in life. It is essential for every human being to discover, understand, and follow their *Dharma*, which will help us live our lives with integrity, success, and fulfillment. When we embody our *Dharma*, we contribute positively to the harmony of the universe, having correctly played our assigned part in the cosmic symphony.

However, many find themselves disconnected from their true *Dharma* due to the demands of modern life. External influences and relentless distractions can cloud our understanding, leading us astray from our authentic path. The Bhagavad Gita reminds us of the importance of *Mama Dharma*—My *Dharma*. By urging deep self-introspection and keen analysis of the world, it helps us rediscover our purpose and realign with the cosmic order.

The Bhagavad Gita encourages us to recognize and embody our unique life purpose and harmonize it with the universal principles of *Dharma*. By understanding the true meaning of *Dharma*, we attune to the infallible divine guidance that promises to lead us toward a life of purpose, integrity, and lasting harmony.

> *"By embracing Dharma, we tune into the grand symphony of the universe."*

Diagnosing Obstacles

Our world is ever-changing and transient. And yet, we unceasingly strive for permanent happiness in these temporary surroundings. We yearn to express our best selves. However, we are often caught unawares by the sudden curve balls life throws at us. We are unable to tackle them and become helpless victims of our circumstances. Why? The Bhagavad Gita offers valuable insights into some innate human weaknesses that hinder us at the most inopportune moments and prevent us from realizing our true potential. A problem understood is a problem half-solved. Once we gain clarity on what obstructs our worldly success and spiritual growth, we can work toward overcoming it.

Mala: Mental Impurities and Binding Tendencies

Mala, mental impurities, and binding tendencies take hold of our minds, obscure our thoughts, and wrongly influence our actions. These mental impurities create anxiety, and despair, and shrink our overall perspective. They weaken our ability to think freely and make conscious choices. *Mala* entraps us in repetitive patterns, stunts our growth, and thus prevents us from reaching our full potential.

Vikshepa: Mental Turbulence and Lack of Focus

Vikshepa, mental turbulence, and lack of focus ruin our concentration. Our wandering thoughts and fluctuating emotions impede our decision-making ability. *Vikshepa* decreases our productivity and efficacy, making it difficult, if not impossible, for us to achieve our goals and experience a sense of fulfillment.

Avarana: Veil of Ignorance

Avarana, the veil of ignorance, prevents us from understanding our true nature and distorts our perception of ourselves and our priorities. This lack of self-awareness distances us from our genuine desires and aspirations. As a result, we chase after superficial goals that do not align with our deepest values, leading to confusion and a disconnection from the truth of our being. *Avarana* jams our access to genuine inner fulfillment and happiness, due to which we continue to frantically seek external sources of joy only to find them fleeting and unsatisfying.

Furthermore, this veil of ignorance blurs our intellectual understanding and prevents us from making informed choices that align with our authentic selves. External influences or societal expectations, rather than our own wisdom and power of discernment, run our lives. Recognition of this obstacle initiates in us the urgent need to overcome this ignorance through Self-discovery so that we can reconnect with our true nature and experience the unlimited joy that springs from absolute clarity in our lives.

Powerful Techniques to Overcome the Obstacles

The Bhagavad Gita equips us with powerful techniques that will lead us from inefficiency and suffering to a state of efficiency and contentment. Diligent employment of these time-tested methods assures personal development and Self-Realization.

Karma Yoga: Dissolving Mental Impurities

Karma Yoga, the path of action, takes care of mental impurities or *mala*. By engaging in worldly activities with the right attitude and in a spirit of service and sacrifice, we purify our minds and transcend the limitations imposed by attachment and ego. Through *Karma Yoga*, we become more compassionate, selfless, and in tune with our true nature.

Upasana Yoga: Cultivating a Powerful and Focused Mind

Upasana Yoga, the path of meditation and devotion, ensures the development of a robust and concentrated mind necessary for success in all endeavors. We learn to overcome *Vikshepa* by harnessing our mental energies and cultivating unwavering focus through various practices such as meditation, mantra repetition, and devotional rituals. A calm and steady mind developed by the sincere practice of *Upasana Yoga* empowers us to overcome life's challenges with clarity, resilience, and a deep sense of purpose.

Jnana Yoga: Dispelling the Veil of Ignorance

Jnana Yoga, the path of knowledge and wisdom, helps lift *Avarana*, the veil of ignorance that shrouds our understanding of our true nature. We strip down layers of ignorance through systematic study and self-inquiry and gain insightful knowledge of our true selves. *Jnana Yoga* enables us to break through illusions, merge with our divine essence, and attain Self-Realization. It liberates us from suffering and uncovers the boundless potential within.

"Diligently use the time-tested techniques taught by the Bhagavad Gita to raise yourself from the depths of suffering to the heights of ultimate efficiency and contentment and let shine the true essence of your Being."

Structure of the Bhagavad Gita

The Bhagavad Gita, a lyrical masterpiece of 701 verses spread across 18 chapters, was initially composed in the ancient Sanskrit language. Its verses rest upon a remarkable framework embellished with profound wisdom and invaluable guidance. Exploring the underlying structure of this sacred scripture enables us to attain a holistic understanding of its essence.

Unraveling the Meters: *Anushtubh* and *Tristubh*

The poetic beauty of the Bhagavad Gita cascades through the interchanging rhythm of two primary meters: *Anushtubh* and *Tristubh*. The *Anushtubh* meter, consisting of four lines of eight syllables each, lends its vibrant pattern to most of the Gita's enchanting verses. This revered form of poetry, a patent meter in epics and sacred texts, imparts a harmonious cadence to the verses.

In moments of heightened drama and emotional intensity, the verses gracefully transition to the *Tristubh* meter. Originating from the Vedic tradition, the four lines of eleven syllables that form this meter create a sense of grandeur, infusing pivotal verses with a resounding impact. These poetic crescendos arrest our attention and stir our hearts to synch with the profundity of the teaching about to be imparted.

The Structure of the Bhagavad Gita

The intriguing flow of the Bhagavad Gita demonstrates a deliberate arrangement that systematically guides seekers along their spiritual path. To begin with, Chapter 1 declares the problem statement, where the Gita addresses the fundamental human problem within the context of an ancient civil war. This chapter sets the stage for the enlightening teachings that follow, directing us to identify the challenges we face in our lives – a step that must precede any transformation.

Chapter 2 is an overview of the entire teachings of the Bhagavad Gita. It serves as a lighthouse that sheds light upon the vast ocean of wisdom that lies ahead.

From Chapter 3 to Chapter 17, the Gita meticulously elaborates upon the principles introduced in Chapter 2. Step-by-step, it delivers clear insights and practical guidance to meet life's challenges. Each chapter thoroughly explains various aspects of human existence and spiritual growth. As we traverse this expansive landscape of knowledge, we discover the multifaceted nature of our being and the perplexing interplay between the inner and outer worlds.

Finally, Chapter 18 consolidates the knowledge gained through the preceding chapters and thoroughly reinforces the central message of the Gita. It puts us face-to-face with a synthesis of wisdom and a call to action, urging us to embody and integrate the teachings of the Bhagavad Gita into our lives.

This method of consolidation, akin to modern management presentations, begins with a summary (Chapter 2), followed by detailed elaboration (Chapters 3-17), and concludes with a comprehensive recap (Chapter 18). It ensures clarity and understanding, as seen in highly effective contemporary communication styles.

The Bhagavad Gita is considered a more relatable exposition of the ancient Upanishads. Divided into three sections, known as *shatkas*, it weaves its subject matter around the Upanishadic aphorism or *Mahavakya - Tat Tvam Asi*, meaning "That thou art." This precise classification offers a sounder understanding of Gita's elemental design.

The first *shatka*, comprising Chapters 1 to 6, focuses primarily on the nature of the individual (*Tvam* - Thou). Here, we explore the depths of our being by contemplating our true nature and the role of self-effort in realizing our highest potential. *Karma Yoga*, the path of selfless action, and the significance of individual effort lay the foundation for our personal growth.

The second *shatka*, spanning Chapters 7 to 12, disentangles the mysteries around the Lord of the Universe (*Tat* – That). Through *Upasana Yoga*, the path of devotion and meditation, we deepen our knowledge of the omnipresence, omnipotence, and omniscience of the Divine. This section emphasizes the importance of cultivating a focused and steadfast mind and gaining mastery over our thoughts. It also sheds light on the role of grace in our spiritual journey and invites us to open our hearts to the ceaseless flow of divine blessings.

The third *shatka*, Chapters 13 to 18, reveals our oneness with the Divine (*Asi* - Art). Here, the path of knowledge, *Jnana Yoga*, takes center stage as we investigate the deeper truths of existence. These chapters emphasize the importance of embodying spiritual values, which will lead us to transcend the limitations of the ego and merge with the divine essence within.

Each chapter of the Bhagavad Gita is aptly called *yoga* to emphasize its transformative power. Yoga has its root in the Sanskrit word *yuj*, which means 'to join or control.' This sacred scripture offers physical, mental, intellectual, and spiritual practices that help us effortlessly connect with higher realms within ourselves.

Our intention is to scrutinize each topic and study each verse from a subjective and objective angle. A thorough understanding gained through such an approach will help us effortlessly utilize these profound learnings in our lives.

"Wading through the Bhagavad Gita's 701 Verses spread across 18 chapters, we begin to slowly glean the irrefutable intimacy between our inner and outer worlds."

A Brief History of the Bhagavad Gita: Its Origins and Evolution

A title like "History of the Gita" is misleading, as the teachings of the Bhagavad Gita go beyond time and historical contexts. When we speak of the history of the Gita, we only refer to its poeticized structural composition, which emerged at a specific point in time. Its teachings on the universal order and the eternal laws governing life have existed since time immemorial and will continue to endure. For example, the famous equation E = mc^2 was documented at a particular time, but its underlying principles were always present. Just as scientific laws are everlasting truths waiting to be discovered, the inexhaustible wisdom of the Bhagavad Gita has been awaiting its revelation in poetic verses to be carefully studied and passed down through generations.

The Bhagavad Gita has its origins in the Mahabharata, the longest epic known to humanity. While the exact timing of the Mahabharata is elusive, scholars estimate that it dates to between 2000 and 6000 years ago. The Gita is an inspiring dialogue between the Universal Teacher, *Bhagavan* Shri Krishna, and the regal warrior Arjuna at the zero hours of battle. Arjuna finds himself incapacitated by overwhelming emotions as he faces his loved and revered ones arrayed against him on the battlefield. He is slumped on the chariot floor, confused about whether he must fight a righteous war or retreat. Sage Vyasa, the venerable seer of ancient times, strategically embedded Krishna's life-transforming instructions within this intense conversation between a dejected seeker and an enlightened master. The Bhagavad Gita beats at the very heart of this grand saga, encapsulating themes of love, heroism, and duty, and resonates with seekers across all time and space.

For centuries, the Bhagavad Gita's wisdom lay somewhat obscured, tucked away within the vast verses of the Mahabharata. Its 701 verses, a mere drop in the ocean of the epic's 85,000, struggled for recognition. Understanding the unfathomable worth and value of this yet undiscovered portion, the great master Adi Shankaracharya, in the 8th century A.D., took on the monumental task of meticulously extracting the Bhagavad Gita from the depths of the mammoth epic and presenting it as an independent scripture. His astounding effort was pivotal to ensure that the Gita's teachings could be accessed and contemplated in their purest form. Shankaracharya wrote a comprehensive commentary on the Bhagavad Gita. He distilled its complex ideas into lucid explanations and made the Gita's revolutionary insights more widely accessible. To this day, Shankaracharya's commentaries remain a trusted guide for those teaching and studying the Gita, testifying that its relevance endures in traditional and contemporary discourses.

Building upon Shankaracharya's legacy, numerous Sanskrit commentaries were written on the Bhagavad Gita, each presenting unique interpretations of its profound teachings. These commentaries, written by respected teachers and visionaries, shed light on the essentials of the Gita from their own metaphysical and experiential vantage points. The uniqueness of the Bhagavad Gita is its versatility; it supports various interpretations, offering rich, multi-faceted insights that enhance our comprehension of its eternal wisdom in a way that resonates with our preferences. Commentaries by luminaries such as Ramanujacharya, Madhavacharya, Abhinava Gupta, Sridhara Swami, and Vallabhacharya have each highlighted distinctive aspects of the Gita, adding to its ever-evolving body of wisdom.

While Sanskrit commentaries facilitated a deeper engagement with the Gita, they remained confined to scholars and inaccessible to non-academicians for centuries. However, the compassionate Sant Jnaneshwar stepped forward to bridge this gap by offering a remarkable Marathi translation called Jnaneshwari. Jnaneshwar's efforts marked a significant milestone in disseminating the wisdom of the Gita, making it available to a broader spectrum of spiritual seekers. Inspired by this noble endeavor, more translations of the Gita began to emerge in various Indian languages, gradually impacting the lives of people across the diverse landscapes of India.

Gita's Journey to the West

Alongside gaining momentum across the Indian subcontinent, the enlightening wisdom of the Bhagavad Gita eventually found its way to the Western world through English translations. Here is the fascinating story of Gita's travel to the West, its initial reception, and its significant impact on Western literature and thought.

Warren Hastings, the British statesperson and Governor General of British India recognized the transformative potential of the Gita. He declared that its study and practice could lead humanity to enduring peace and contentment, surpassing even beyond the era of British rule in India [12]. Encouraged by Hastings, Charles Wilkins, an employee of the British East India Company, accomplished the monumental feat of translating the Bhagavad Gita into English in 1785.

The Bhagavad Gita gradually began to capture the imagination of Western scholars and intellectuals. It sparked intrigue among English Orientalists, German Romantics, and American Transcendentalists alike. Readers could effortlessly relate to the contents of the Gita due to its thorough amalgamation of spirituality and practical wisdom that connected so perfectly with real-life experiences.

With global interest in the practical application of the Gita growing, translations began to emerge in various European languages, including French, Russian, German, and Latin. As these translations began to defy cultural and linguistic boundaries, the Gita became more recognized as scriptural and intellectual literature rather than mere poetry or a song. With its practical relevance resonating profoundly, the Bhagavad Gita saw a surge in popularity among Western seekers of inspiration and spiritual depth in the late 19th century.

Wilkins's translation was pivotal in introducing the Gita to Western scholars and making it popular among American transcendentalists [12]. It helped shape the transcendentalist movement in America. Ralph Waldo Emerson, the renowned transcendentalist philosopher who received a copy of Wilkins's translation from Thomas Carlyle, considered the Gita his wellspring of inspiration. Henry David Thoreau, another prominent transcendentalist, gained immense learning and solace from the profound philosophy of the Gita.

In the late 19th century, the Gita experienced a translation surge and began to occupy a new cultural space. Scholars and intellectuals focused on the allegorical and symbolic aspects of the text, highlighting its universal relevance beyond its Indian origins. Sir Edwin Arnold's compelling translation, "The Song Celestial" (1885), was widely read and influenced Western readers' perception of the Gita.

Theosophist and spiritual teacher Helena Blavatsky [13] drew upon the timeless wisdom of the Gita for her works, exalting the universality of its teachings. The poet W.B. Yeats [14] acknowledged the Bhagavad Gita as a source of inspiration and drew parallels between its ideas and his own spiritual journey.

Swami Vivekananda, the renowned Indian monk and spiritual leader, played a crucial role in introducing the Bhagavad Gita to the Western world through his 1983 lecture series in America. His extraordinary insights and passionate delivery captivated audiences. Swami Vivekananda's efforts sparked a renewed interest in the Bhagavad Gita and further enhanced its reputation as a revered scripture and a powerhouse of spiritual wisdom.

The influence of the Bhagavad Gita continued to spread through the 20th century. In the 1920s, Paramahamsa Yogananda, a spiritual leader and founder of the Self-Realization Fellowship, introduced the Western world to the wonders of Kriya Yoga. His widely acclaimed book, Autobiography of a Yogi, brought some unknown spiritual perspectives into the world for the very first time. His masterful commentary on the Bhagavad Gita, *God Talks with Arjuna,* perfectly connected the principles of *Kriya Yoga* to the core teachings of the Bhagavad Gita. By correlating the two paths of *Kriya Yoga* and *Jnana Yoga*, he proved the

Bhagavad Gita's role and relevance in any seeker's spiritual upliftment, irrespective of the path chosen.

Another noteworthy figure was A.C. Bhakti Vedanta Swami Prabhupada, the founder of the International Society for Krishna Consciousness (ISKCON). In the 1960s and 1970s, he brought the Bhagavad Gita and the teachings of *Bhagavan* Shri Krishna to the West, establishing ISKCON temples and spreading Krishna consciousness across the globe.

During this time, Maharishi Mahesh Yogi, the founder of Transcendental Meditation, propagated the practical application of the Bhagavad Gita to promote inner peace and well-being. His meditation and spirituality courses aligned well with the vision of the Bhagavad Gita, further facilitating Western seekers' relatability to the Gita.

Today, the Bhagavad Gita's influence clearly extends beyond its traditional boundaries. Its timeless wisdom has permeated Western literature, philosophy, and thought, transforming the minds and hearts of countless individuals who seek a higher purpose in life. In and through the world's growing interconnectedness, the Gita inspires and guides seekers worldwide on their spiritual quests. It has become a beloved and respected source of knowledge, guidance, and motivation for humanity.

The Bhagavad Gita's Role in the Indian Independence Movement

The Bhagavad Gita played a pivotal role in India's quest for independence. Chatrapati Shivaji Maharaj, a revered Maratha warrior known for his exceptional bravery and courage in and through his encounters with various invasions, drew inspiration from the Gita to pursue his dream of *Swarajya—the* independence of his beloved Bharat. When confronted with complex administrative challenges, he and his mother, Jijabai, frequently turned to the verses of the Bhagavad Gita for guidance.

During the early 20th century, nationalists recognized the Gita as a source of inspiration and guidance through their arduous pursuit of freedom [15]. The Gita's assertive teachings of duty, righteousness, and selfless action perfectly served the aspirations of the Indian people and instilled in them a sense of purpose and determination.

The Swadeshi movement exemplified the influence of the Gita on the freedom struggle, arising in response to the oppressive policies of the British colonial government. Thousands of Indians pledged to boycott British goods and exclusively support indigenous products. They undertook a historic march to the Kali Temple in Kolkata, carrying copies of the Bhagavad Gita. This act demonstrated their dedication to the Gita's doctrines of self-reliance, national unity, and resistance against injustice.

The British authorities perceived the Bhagavad Gita as a potent symbol of Indian nationalism and resistance against colonial rule. Possessing more than one copy of the Gita became a cause for suspicion, as the British feared its potential to ignite patriotic fervor and rouse acts of defiance. This further highlights the indisputable impact of the Gita on the collective consciousness of the Indian people, as well as its recognition as an influential force in empowering their struggle for independence.

The Bhagavad Gita was a mighty source of inspiration for prominent freedom fighters during India's struggle for independence. Lokmanya Tilak, hailed as the "Father of Indian Unrest," kept stressing the practicality of the teachings of the Bhagavad Gita and urged the Indian people to understand its message. While igniting religious and nationalistic fervor through his writings, Bankim Chandra Chatterjee found in the Gita the ideal for humanity to embody. Mahatma Gandhi, whose name is synonymous with India's independence, found reassurance within the verses of the Gita in times of despair while advocating for non-violent resistance. Sri Aurobindo Ghose recognized the critical role of the Gita in uplifting human consciousness and liberating humanity from its lower nature. These remarkable leaders and visionaries found enormous courage and strength in the ageless wisdom of the Bhagavad Gita, which fueled their quest for freedom and dramatically altered the trajectory of Indian history.

In addition to these notable leaders, the Bhagavad Gita influenced many others in India's struggle for independence. For instance, freedom fighters like Damodar Chapekar, Madanlal Dhingra, Khudiram Bose, and Hemu Kalani relied on the Gita as their constant companion during their final days of life, substantiating the uplifting impact of its teachings on their spirits and actions.

The Bhagavad Gita furnished the intellectual and spiritual foundation for India's freedom movement. Its message of selfless action, moral courage, and the pursuit of truth aligned perfectly with leaders and revolutionaries who sought to liberate their nation from colonial rule. The Gita became a way-shower, motivating individuals to uphold their principles and dedicate themselves to the cause of freedom. The influence of the Gita helped formulate the strategies and approaches adopted in India's struggle for independence.

Gita's Torch Kept Ablaze: Swami Chinmayananda and Swami Dayananda's Legacy

Two great luminaries, Swami Chinmayananda and Swami Dayananda Sarasvati, played a crucial role in bringing the perennial teachings of the Gita to the forefront by magnifying its wisdom through the lens of Advaita Vedanta in the modern era.

Swami Chinmayananda's legacy as one of the most dynamic and influential teachers of the Bhagavad Gita in contemporary times is unparalleled. After being initiated onto the spiritual path by Swami Sivananda, he spent time in the Himalayas with Swami Tapovan Maharaj to deepen his scriptural understanding. Returning from the Himalayas, he delivered his first public lecture on Vedanta in English on December 31, 1951, in Pune, India. English was not the medium of Vedantic instruction in India at the time. The shocked traditionalists brutally opposed it. On the first day, there were only four people in the audience, which grew to a few thousand by the final day of the lecture series. He resolved to undertake the remarkable mission of initiating the tradition of *Jnana Yagnas*, a series of enlightening discourses in English to spread the wisdom of Vedanta and the Bhagavad Gita worldwide. There was no looking back after that. With his eloquent and electrifying talks, Swami Chinmayananda captivated the minds and intellects of modern, educated English-speaking individuals of all ages from varied strata of society, setting them on a quest for scriptural understanding and abidance, sincere service to humanity, and self-realization.

Swami Chinmayananda also established Sandeepany Sadhanalaya, an academy dedicated to teaching the vision of Vedanta. This institution remains a sacred conduit for perpetuating spiritual education, ensuring the torch of knowledge passes to future generations.

Similarly, Swami Dayananda Saraswati was a luminous spiritual presence in the modern era. His dedication to preserving and disseminating the traditional teachings of Advaita Vedanta in a contemporary setting earned him exceptional respect and reverence. Swami Dayananda Saraswati's brilliance shone through his clear understanding of the subject and his ability to create a lineage of teachers who could carry the torch of knowledge forward.

While Swami Chinmayananda illuminated the path for seekers from all levels of society, Swami Dayananda Saraswati emerged as a teacher of teachers, empowering countless individuals with the wisdom of Advaita Vedanta.

They both carried the knowledge of the Bhagavad Gita into everyday life by introducing the concept of Gita Study Classes run by and for householders. Today, countless families worldwide are blessed with a weekly collective study of the Bhagavad Gita. Within the context of the Mahabharata storyline, the divine dialogue of the Gita transpired between one *grihastha* (householder) and another *grihastha* (householder) on the battlefield of Kurukshetra, which is symbolically akin to ordinary human beings trying to master the playing field of life under the guidance of the scriptures. These outstanding spiritual educators brought the Gita back to its rightful place, where it would be of maximum use.

The journey of the Bhagavad Gita continues unimpeded in this digital age because of the contributions of these two outstanding masters. Swami Chinmayananda and Swami Dayananda Saraswati stand as exemplars of spiritual enlightenment that illuminate striving intellects with the wisdom of the ancient scriptures. Their unprecedented efforts have ensured that the age-old yet forever-relevant teachings of the Bhagavad Gita continue to guide modern-day seekers toward self-discovery. The resounding impact of these extraordinary teachers echoes keenly through the pages of this book and the hearts of the entire team at Project Self.

The Enduring Legacy of the Bhagavad Gita in the 2020s

In and through the dynamic struggles and victories of the 2020s, the immortal wisdom of the Bhagavad Gita continues to fascinate and transform many intellects worldwide. Now being actively propagated by spiritual leaders and revered teachers like Swami Sarvapriyananda and Swami Tadatmananda, among others, the wisdom of the Bhagavad Gita is becoming increasingly relevant for modern seekers.

In recent notable events, Tulsi Gabbard, the former United States Congresswoman, took her oath of office by placing her hand on the Bhagavad Gita, reflecting the growing strength of the scripture on international platforms.

The philosophy of the Bhagavad Gita has also profoundly touched the psyche of the entertainment industry. The renowned musician George Harrison of the Beatles found comfort and inspiration in the verses of the Gita. He began infusing its timeless wisdom into his music, illustrating how seamlessly Gita's teachings percolate through artistic disciplines.

An extraordinary movie starring Will Smith and directed by Robert Redford (2000), based on Steven Pressfield's 1995 book The Legend of Bagger Vance: A Novel of Golf and the Game of Life, brought the Bhagavad Gita hugely under the spotlight. The plot is loosely but most undeniably based on the teachings of the Bhagavad Gita. It depicts Will Smith (Bagger Vance) coaching one-time great golfer Matt Damon (R. Junuh) out of his gut-wrenching despondency to superstardom again. Much like Shri Krishna brought Arjuna out of his incapacitating despair, The verses of the Gita can be seen echoing through the game's instructions. After the release of this movie, which was a tremendous success at the box office, Will Smith developed a personal affinity for the Bhagavad Gita and cites it several times in his speeches worldwide. The movie has proven to be an effective tool in many spiritual youth workshops to further simplify the lofty tenets of the Bhagavad Gita.

The Bhagavad Gita is famously known to have influenced political leaders as well. Rishi Sunak, the British Conservative Party politician, publicly credits the Gita as a source of inspiration. Indian Prime Minister Narendra Modi is also consistently vocal about his interest in the vision of the Gita and often gifts copies of the sacred scripture to foreign dignitaries during official engagements.

In recent years, the popularity of the Bhagavad Gita has been increasing within traditional spiritual communities and regions beyond its cultural origins, including Latin America and Africa. Latin America has witnessed a growing interest in the Bhagavad Gita, with many individuals and spiritual groups adopting its teachings. Yoga studios, meditation centers, and philosophical circles introducing the principles of the Bhagavad Gita to spiritual enthusiasts seeking inner peace are on the rise. Scholars and academicians in Latin American universities are also investigating the philosophical and cultural significance of the Gita to determine its potential influence on contemporary societies.

The Bhagavad Gita has also found a receptive audience in Africa. Spiritual seekers and practitioners are drawn to its pragmatic wisdom, which relates well to the human spirit. The Gita's universal theme that stresses duty, righteousness, and selfless action has struck a chord with Africans seeking a deeper understanding of their spiritual heritage and a quest for meaning.

The relevance of the Bhagavad Gita has not gone unnoticed in academic and corporate arenas. Celebrated universities across the globe have integrated the study of the Gita into their philosophy, religious studies, and humanities curricula. Scholars and researchers have closely examined its philosophical yet logical teachings and affirmed its impact on ethical decision-making and human consciousness.

In the corporate world, the principles of the Bhagavad Gita have been adopted by forward-thinking leaders who recognize the value of its wisdom in fostering virtuous leadership, employee well-being, and sustainable business practices. Many prominent corporations have integrated Gita-inspired concepts into their leadership training programs as they recognize the potential of its teachings to create and nurture resilient and compassionate leaders.

As the influence of the Bhagavad Gita continues to gain momentum worldwide, its teachings continue to be a source of inspiration, solace, and transformation for people across continents. Its universal appeal lies in its capacity to address the fundamental questions of human existence, offering revolutionary insights devoid of cultural or geographical constraints. Whether in the classrooms of prestigious universities or in the hearts of individuals seeking purpose and fulfillment, the Bhagavad Gita remains an eternal lighthouse of wisdom, ushering humanity toward the calm shores of self-discovery and harmonious coexistence.

"The Bhagavad Gita's teachings echo an everlasting sonnet of hope, courage, and wisdom across all time and space."

The Art of Studying the Bhagavad Gita

The Bhagavad Gita holds a special place in the hearts of countless individuals worldwide. From providing solace in times of distress to offering intellectual gratification through its logic-imbued messages, Gita's teachings have been embraced by people in numerous ways. However, it is worth pondering: Are we genuinely reaping the maximum benefits from the Gita, or are we merely scratching the surface of its unfathomable vision and scope?

For some, reading the Gita may be a part of their daily ritualistic routine, a form of prayer-recitation. Some others may be devotionally, even superstitiously, attached to it. Many turn to its wisdom for an emotional boost or intellectual guidance during challenging times. Some people born into the Hindu culture are naturally connected to the Gita as part of their upbringing. Scholars and academicians may stand agape at Gita's ability to impart the highest philosophical truths through mesmerizing poetry or find a thrill in decoding the enigmatic principles of the text. Not to mention, a few cynics may read the Gita out of curiosity to solely question and challenge its teachings.

Yet, the Bhagavad Gita is far more than an object of devotion or a mere intellectual pursuit. It is a book of utmost practicality that offers transformative insights to systematically keep elevating us to the next best version of ourselves. Not only do the teachings of the Gita guide us step-by-step on our spiritual journey, but they help us live a life of prosperity and contentment. To unlock its inherent power, we must rethink and refine how we approach the study of the Gita.

The life-transforming tenets of the Gita have often been likened to milk drawn from a cow. The cow that feeds on inedible raw grass symbolizes the Upanishads. Its milk signifies the easily digested version of the otherwise cryptic philosophy of the Upanishads. Krishna, the compassionate milkman, milked out this divine nectar from its inaccessible depths, not just for Arjuna, who is represented by the calf - but for all humankind. Think! The calf drinks little of the cow's milk; most of the milk goes on to feed entire communities. And what is the purpose of milk? Does it merely invoke awe and admiration from within us, or is it meant for consumption and nourishment?

In the same way, simply glorifying and worshipping the Gita will not lead to spiritual evolution. Just as milk nourishes and sustains the body, the Gita nourishes and transforms our inner being. Its miraculous potency is witnessed and experienced when we make these teachings an integral and indispensable part of our lives. When this timeless wisdom percolates through our decisions, actions, and relationships, the true power of the Gita is unleashed from within and around us.

Many take up the study of the Bhagavad Gita as an intellectual challenge and become proficient in remembering and parroting its awe-inspiring content. In doing so, they undoubtedly become erudite scholars and appear as walking encyclopedias of the subject to a world teeming with enthusiastic seekers. However, the fundamental objective of this divine vision lies beyond intellectual mastery. The true purpose of studying the Gita is to access, understand, and imbibe its core message and discover the Self.

A Methodical Approach to Studying and Mastering the Bhagavad Gita

The beauty of the Vedantic tradition lies not only in the insights it offers into the nature of our existence but also in its wondrous teaching methodology. A three-step approach prescribed by the Vedanta tradition: Systematic study (*Shravanam*), Contemplation (*Mananam*), Analysis, and Internalization through practice (*Nidhidhyasanam*) facilitates our understanding of this otherwise complex text.

Step 1: Systematic Study (*Shravanam*)

As new initiates on the spiritual path, we begin to realize our ignorance, and so "we seek to know." The first step on this transformative journey is the systematic study of the Gita, known as *Shravanam*. This entails consistently and diligently immersing ourselves in the exploration of the sacred verses under the guidance of a competent teacher. A true teacher acts as a torchbearer, skillfully unfolding and connecting the teachings of the Gita to real-life experiences. The wisdom of the Gita comes alive through the sacred interaction between teacher and student.

Through this phase, we are encouraged to seek clarity and not give in to blind acceptance. The Gita invites us to ponder over and question its teachings deeply. This quintessential first step lays the foundation for a profound understanding that transcends mere intellectual grasping.

Step 2: Contemplation and Analysis (*Mananam*)

So now "we know," but "we do not fully understand." The second step, *mananam*, calls for personally analyzing the knowledge we received through *shravanam*, or systematic study, and becomes possible only through consistent mental churning and contemplation. We are urged to dissect the teachings, connect the dots between their verses, and bridge the gap between learned philosophy and the life we experience in our world. This non-negotiable phase is a dynamic dialogue between our intellect and the teachings of the Gita that helps clarify any lingering doubts.

We are encouraged to consistently re-engage with our teacher to pose questions and gain further clarification to refine our understanding. While our teachers continue to guide us, *mananam* is a phase we must necessarily navigate in relative solitude. A doctor may prescribe medicine, but we must consume it ourselves for it to work. Similarly, while knowledge can be passed on, authentic wisdom flourishes through our internal contemplation and ability to apply these teachings to our everyday lives. *Mananam* is that transformative phase where knowledge is given time and space to mature into wisdom.

Step 3: Internalization through Practice (*Nidhidhyasanam*)

Owing to the first two steps, we now "know" and "understand." But "we have not yet internalized." To gain a personal experience of what we know and understand and to validate for ourselves the pragmatic truth of this philosophy, the third step, *Nidhidhyasanam*, beckons us to assimilate the teachings of the Gita into the very fabric of our being. It is here that we internalize the knowledge gained. Like drops of rain merging with the ocean, we allow the teachings, one at a time, to become an inseparable part of us. This is only possible through consistently putting into practice what we have studied. Remember, it is only practice that makes perfect.

This internalization must follow intellectual knowing and understanding and permeate our thoughts, feelings, words, and actions. As the fragrance of the teachings infuses every aspect of our lives, we begin to embody and live the profound essence of the Bhagavad Gita. Through this process, the Gita empowers us to navigate life's challenges with deep inner wisdom, compassion, and resilience. We begin to unleash our highest potential.

The transformative power of the Bhagavad Gita lies not in passive reading but in active engagement. By faithfully employing the three-step approach of systematic study (*Shravanam*), contemplation (*Mananam*), and internalization through practice (*Nidhidhyasam*), we unlock the hidden doors to spiritual growth and Self-Realization. This journey of Self-discovery becomes more meaningful when you begin to know, understand, and experience the power of its teachings firsthand.

> *"The wisdom of the Bhagavad Gita yields not to those who look on in idle admiration but to those who uncompromisingly devote themselves to the study, understanding, and integration of its sacred verses."*

Challenges on the Path

An in-depth study of a scriptural text like the Bhagavad Gita is not bereft of challenges and can appear daunting to many. Let us closely examine some of these challenges.

1. Maintaining Clarity amidst Diverse Interpretations

The Bhagavad Gita, with its highly esoteric insights into Absolute Reality and the true nature of mortal existence, is no ordinary text to interpret. Beyond the boundaries of space, time, and causation, its sheer vastness renders it an obscure body of wisdom that falls outside the grasp of human understanding. The profundity that enriches the Gita presents us with our first challenge: the diversity in interpretations of its teachings.

Like all other Vedantic teachings, the Bhagavad Gita opens itself to various scholarly perspectives, depending on which school of thought is interpreting it. *Dvaita* (Duality), *Vishishtadvaita* (Qualified Monism), and *Advaita* (Monism) each hold a unique lens through which the Gita's teachings are understood and expounded. For instance, the followers of *Dvaita* consider *Bhagavan* as the source of the universe and individuals, believing in a separation between the individual and the Divine. *Vishishtadvaita* followers view the individual as a part of the whole, professing the path of devotion (*Bhakti*) to liberation. While the *Advaita* tradition perceives the essential oneness of the individual and the Divine, seeking liberation through the path of knowledge (*Jnana*).

The following story illustrates this point perfectly:

Sri Rama asked Hanuman, 'Who am I to you?'

Hanuman replied, "Oh Lord, as long as I identify with my body, I am your servant.

When my intelligence transcends the material world and I think spiritually, I become a part of you.

And when I elevate my consciousness to the spiritual plane, you and I are one and the same."

These viewpoints, though diverse, are all valid. Much like different facets of a vast ocean. Just as a wave can be seen as a child of the ocean, a part of the ocean, or even as the ocean itself, the teachings of the

Bhagavad Gita resonate with seekers in unique ways aligned to their personal inclinations and spiritual backgrounds. However, herein lies the challenge: confusion inadvertently arises when an unseasoned seeker, following a particular path, encounters commentaries or teachings from a different school of thought. Contradicting interpretations from varying perspectives perplex the student's mind.

To overcome this challenge, it is vital for seekers to identify the commentary and teaching methodology that resonate most strongly with them. Being guided by a competent teacher and supported by a group of people sharing the same resonance is critical at this stage. Sticking to that perspective until a thorough understanding is attained ensures clarity and coherence in the study process. A deep comprehension within the context of the chosen approach is essential—every aspect of the teaching should make sense.

In conclusion, the challenge posed by one's inability to reconcile different interpretations of the Bhagavad Gita can be overcome through wisdom, discernment, and dedication to choosing a path that one feels most aligned with. By focusing on a chosen viewpoint for a period, seeking guidance and support from competent guides and study groups, and refraining from prematurely blending multiple commentaries, we can avoid this often-insurmountable obstacle along our path.

2. Accurate Comprehension of the Sanskrit Language to Avoid Misinterpretations

Any text, whether scriptural or otherwise, is best understood in the language of its conception. The Bhagavad Gita was originally written in Sanskrit. This ancient, beautiful, but extraordinarily complex language is by far the most difficult to translate, especially while trying to keep the writings' original and intended meaning intact. It poses a challenge for many contemporary students and teachers of the Gita. Not knowing or not being proficient in Sanskrit often leads to incorrect or incomplete translations and interpretations, which distort the sacred teachings of the scripture.

One major problem in translation is finding direct equivalents for certain Sanskrit words in other languages. This limitation can create subtle yet significant discrepancies in the interpretation of the text. For instance, consider the word *atma*, often translated as 'soul' in English. However, the Western connotation of the word soul is not the true meaning of *atma* in Sanskrit. In Christianity, only humans have souls, whereas the Vedas recognize the existence of *atma* in all living beings, even plants and animals. Such crucial disparities in interpretation can result in considerable miscommunication of the actual message of the Gita.

The context-sensitive nature of Sanskrit words adds another layer of complicatedness. For example, as seen earlier, the word *Dharma* possesses multiple meanings, such as duty, religion, essential law, and more. In many translations, *Dharma* is interpreted solely as religion, which dilutes the all-encompassing immensity of the Gita's vision.

To overcome this challenge effectively, students of the Gita must seek guidance from teachers who have received training from the traditional Vedanta lineage. By communicating the precise meanings of the verses, these qualified teachers keep the message's authenticity intact. Cross-referencing their learnings with traditional commentaries like the famed Adi Shankara will also aid seekers in gaining a holistic understanding of the Bhagavad Gita. Students must also engage their own intelligence and discernment while studying the Gita. They are encouraged to critically analyze the translations and interpretations and align them with the broader vision of the Gita.

In conclusion, while mastering Sanskrit can certainly enhance one's understanding of the Bhagavad Gita, it is not a prerequisite for understanding its universal teachings. Nonproficiency in Sanskrit should not deter anyone from exploring the Gita. Its teachings are meant for anyone aspiring to greater meaning and spiritual insight. Fortunately, with the assistance of qualified teachers, the insights provided by meticulously translated commentaries, and the application of critical thinking, seekers can uncover the Gita's wisdom without being fluent in the Sanskrit language.

3. Balancing Devotion and Intellectual Inquiry

Eternally revered as a sacred scripture, the Gita naturally evokes deep faith and devotion among its readers. However, blind adherence without intellectual inquiry can impede genuine understanding and forestall the realization of its profound teachings.

As we will see in verse 34 of the fourth chapter of the Bhagavad Gita, *Bhagavan* Krishna himself teaches the importance of a balanced approach through one's spiritual quest and encourages seekers to question and contemplate the wisdom presented.

Through the simple gesture of Krishna addressing Arjuna as a friend, we are encouraged to believe in an egalitarian relationship between teacher and student, despite their differing spiritual statures. As students, we need not fear seeking clarification of our doubts or refraining from questioning what we do not understand. The Gita advocates an intellectual curiosity that does not hesitate to investigate the profound truths it expounds.

However, an overly skeptical or pessimistic approach can also hinder the learning process. Approaching the Gita with preconceived notions to dismiss its teachings prevents one from understanding its keen insights. An opposing attitude toward the scripture denies the cynic the transformative possibility of its wisdom.

The solution lies in harmonizing devotion and intellectual inquiry—like two wings that lift the seeker toward higher knowledge. Nurturing faith and reverence while engaging in thoughtful examination ensures a perfect understanding of the text. A balanced approach enables the seeker to study the scripture with a pure heart and a sharp intellect, free from judgment and prejudice.

In conclusion, it is crucial to continually balance devotion and intellectual inquiry while studying the Bhagavad Gita. A spirit of inquiry must temper blind faith, and skepticism should yield to devotional receptivity. By approaching the text in this manner, seekers will grasp the whole truth embedded within the counsel of the Bhagavad Gita and experience its miraculous effects along their spiritual journey.

4. Context Vs. Content

The Bhagavad Gita emerges from the context of a great battle, wherein Arjuna grapples with overwhelming situational pressure. There is a tendency among many to get entangled in the twists and turns of the context and inadvertently focus more on the Mahabharata storyline than the vital messages the Gita intends to impart.

In our pursuit to understand the Gita, our objective should not be to conduct historical research on the events of the Mahabharata but rather to comprehend, imbibe, and apply the teachings to improve the quality of our lives. The Mahabharata battle, Arjuna's specific circumstances, and even Arjuna himself should not become the central focus of our study.

We must recognize that the context of the Gita extends far beyond the historical epic—it is a universal context that reflects all human experiences. Each of us is continually combating various inner and outer struggles. Without exception, we all face physical, emotional, intellectual, professional, and social challenges. The teachings of the Gita are equally, if not more, applicable to these off-the-battlefield contexts.

Drawing a factual parallel, consider how Sir Isaac Newton discovered the law of gravitation. He observed an apple falling and wondered why it fell straight down, not sideways or upwards. The documented specifics of when and where this observation occurred do not alter the fundamental message—the revelation of the law of gravitation. And what are we concerned with? Understanding the law of gravity. Not how he discovered it.

Similarly, becoming overly obsessed with the details of the historical setting of the Bhagavad Gita, such as specific dates, events, or characters, takes away from the vitality of its teachings. We risk losing sight of its timeless wisdom by fixating excessively on its archival backdrop.

This tendency to get entangled with the inconsequential can be overcome by realizing that the wisdom of Gita is not confined to a specific moment in history. Krishna's teachings in the Gita are for each of us. They address our personal and collective struggles and dilemmas.

The Bhagavad Gita rips through the barriers of time and place and reaches out to every human being seeking guidance. We must develop the skill to continually relate every tenet of the Gita to our own lives and thereby use its immortal wisdom to navigate our unique circumstances. In this manner, we unleash the universal applicability of the Bhagavad Gita and make way for its infallible directives to guide us on our journey toward inner growth, abundant life, and Self-discovery.

5. Academic Approach vs. Spiritual Journey

We must recognize that the study of the Bhagavad Gita differs from conventional studies, like exploring subjects such as Physics or Computer Science. While we study Physics to comprehend the laws of the physical world, the study of the Gita serves a higher purpose—it is an expedition into the depths of our being. The Gita's wisdom is not an academic exercise but a spiritual journey of growth and Self-discovery.

Imagine embarking on a road trip armed with a detailed roadmap. As we study the map, we become acquainted with the twists and turns of the route, the scenic stops, and the potential obstacles along the way. However, if we confine ourselves to merely memorizing the map without embarking on the journey, the map remains a lifeless piece of paper. The true value of the roadmap lies in its practical application, guiding us on the journey toward our destination.

Similarly, the Bhagavad Gita is like a sacred roadmap, guiding us through the complex terrain of life's predicaments. Its teachings are useless if confined within the pages of a book. We must integrate them into the very core of our being and relate them to the unfolding of life. Like progressive milestones, every verse offers increasingly profound insights and marks a step forward on our spiritual journey.

To understand this better, let us simply glean over verse 47 of Chapter II, which we will study in detail in the next book of the Gita Odyssey series. Herein, *Bhagavan* Shri Krishna advises Arjuna to perform his duty without binding attachment to the results. This verse guides us to fulfill our responsibilities to the best of our ability without becoming addicted to the outcome. If we memorize this oft-quoted verse but fail to implement it in our daily lives, the wisdom of the Gita remains a beautiful philosophy in our heads but utterly useless in life. Despite knowing the verse by heart, we will continue to be overwhelmed with worry and anxiety about the fruit of our actions.

In conclusion, the study of the Bhagavad Gita goes beyond a mere intellectual pursuit. It is a deliberate excursion into an awareness of the all-pervading Divinity, an understanding of the human personality in the context of the material world, comprehending the connection between the two, and consequent spiritual evolution. Approaching the Gita as a mere textbook, we miss the opportunity to tap into its transformative potential. Instead, we must befriend it as a precious guide and use it as a sacred roadmap to help us navigate life's undulating terrain.

Busting the Myths and Clearing Misunderstandings

The Bhagavad Gita, one of the most revered scriptures in the world, offers eternal wisdom and practical guidance to seekers of truth. Yet, despite its uncontested popularity, misconceptions and myths surrounding it have found their way into the collective consciousness. Some spring from genuine ignorance, while others are purposefully propagated with devious vested interests. Let's take a closer look at them.

1. The Bhagavad Gita is a Religious Text Only for Hindus

One common misconception is that the Bhagavad Gita is a religious text meant exclusively for Hindus. While it originates within the *Sanatana Dharma*, commonly known as Hinduism, its teachings carry universal significance and apply to people from all backgrounds and belief systems. Embracing the Gita's wisdom does not necessitate converting to Hinduism.

At its core, the Gita emphasizes nurturing human potential and understanding the path to Self-Realization, making it relevant to all of humanity. Furthermore, this sacred scripture does not impose any exclusive path to the Divine; it grants complete freedom in how one worships *Ishvara* in any form. The great master Swami Vivekananda eloquently underscored this inclusivity during his historic address at the World Parliament of Religions in 1893, shedding light on the Bhagavad Gita's universal appeal and timeless relevance.

2. The Bhagavad Gita Propagates War and Violence

Owing to gory misinterpretations, the Bhagavad Gita is often condemned as a war-mongering text that propagates violence. This drastically limited perspective takes one farthest away from the real message of the Gita. While it is true that the Gita is presented within the context of a battlefield, it does not condone or encourage any external war. Instead, it provides incredible insights into the human psyche and blesses humanity with highly potent spiritual wisdom that extends far beyond the frontiers of any battlefield. The Mahabharata war symbolizes the unceasing inner battles we encounter throughout our lives. The call of the Bhagavad Gita is to destroy our own lower tendencies that keep us from living our best lives. The external enemy is symbolic of our own negative qualities. There is no one we need to conquer but ourselves!

Mahatma Gandhi, the renowned advocate of non-violence, drew inspiration from the teachings of the Bhagavad Gita to further anchor himself into the principles of peaceful resistance. He held onto the Gita as a guiding light through his journey toward compassion and truth. This alone illustrates that the spirit of the Bhagavad Gita lies not in glorifying war but in illuminating the path of righteous action, selfless devotion, and inner transformation.

The Bhagavad Gita educates humanity to persevere through life's trials and struggles. It gives its students tremendous strength to confront dilemmas, make ethical choices, and attain inner harmony amidst chaos. The counsel given to the warrior Arjuna on the battlefield universally applies to every individual aspiring for personal development and Self-Realization.

3. The Bhagavad Gita is a Complex Philosophical Treatise

The Bhagavad Gita is often looked upon as a complex philosophical treatise. It is not mere philosophy but a practical guide to understanding ourselves and living a purposeful life. Some may initially find its teachings daunting, and rightfully so. But as one diligently progresses through study under the guidance of the right teacher, the vision of the Gita becomes increasingly transparent. The Gita begins by presenting itself as a jarring problem statement, highlighting the struggles and strife in human life. Then, it offers a step-by-step program to resolve these challenges. Unlike many religious texts that promise rewards in the afterlife, the Bhagavad Gita emphasizes the transformative power of its teachings in the here and now. The benefits of its teachings are not experienced postmortem but rather attainable in the present moment through sincere study and application in our daily lives. Even the slightest effort in applying its wisdom can yield outstanding results, leading to inner harmony, personal growth, and a deeper connection with the Self.

4. The Bhagavad Gita Advocates Renunciation of Action

One prevalent misconception about the Bhagavad Gita is that it advocates renunciation of action, implying that its philosophy is irrelevant for individuals actively involved in worldly life. This belief is far from the truth and completely contradicts the message of the Gita. The battlefield upon which Krishna imparts this life-transforming wisdom to Arjuna is a powerful metaphor, emphasizing that the Gita is meant for those facing life's challenges squarely, which is all of us! It does not even remotely suggest abandoning one's responsibilities or duties.

The brilliance of the Gita lies in its ability to elevate the mundane to the sacred. It elucidates this transformative approach in the third chapter, where Krishna emphasizes the significance of active engagement in life, guided by the right attitude. The Gita does not encourage renunciation in the conventional sense; instead, it teaches us to perform our duties with dedication and sincerity, fueled by a thorough understanding of our interconnectedness with the cosmic order. By adopting this perspective, professionals, householders, and all seekers can integrate spirituality into their daily lives and find fulfillment, purpose, and inner harmony in all worldly endeavors.

The correct understanding of the Bhagavad Gita dispels the myth around renunciation. It emphasizes enlightened action through which the duties and responsibilities of life transform into sacred offerings on the altar of spiritual evolution. It hails the Gita as an infallible guide for those seeking to infuse their lives with meaning and purpose. It offers seekers a pathway to Self-Realization while keeping them astutely engaged with the difficulties of mortal existence.

5. The Bhagavad Gita is a Fatalistic Text

One of the most common misconceptions surrounding the Bhagavad Gita is the erroneous belief that it promotes fatalism, leaving individuals at the mercy of an unalterable destiny governed solely by the law of *karma*. This misinterpretation arises from a very narrow understanding of the law of *karma*. In truth, Gita's teachings on *karma* go far beyond predestined fate.

Karma is not an inescapable web of cosmic determinism; it is the law of cause and effect, emphasizing that our actions have consequences. The Bhagavad Gita places the onus of the quality of our lives right back on our shoulders and not on some judge and jury outside of us.

No doubt, the Bhagavad Gita pairs every effect with its cause and, in a sense, stresses that whatever we meet in life today has its roots in what we have done in the past. But it draws our attention to the fact that how we meet what stands before us today will determine what happens tomorrow. It shows us how, literally, minute by minute, we are the co-creators of our destinies.

The Bhagavad Gita teaches us to primarily acknowledge what is a product of our own past deeds. No matter what circumstance we find ourselves in today, the Gita urges us to now act with wisdom, compassion, and virtuous intention. It shows us how, by aligning our present actions with higher principles and selflessly serving others, we can courageously meet and intelligently transcend the effects of *karma*. Through the lens of the Gita, life is not a mere cosmic lottery but an ever-evolving sum of sound intentions, conscious choices, deliberate actions, and growth that ultimately leads to Self-Realization.

6. The Bhagavad Gita is exclusively for Ascetics and Spiritual Seekers

The Bhagavad Gita is sometimes misunderstood as a scripture exclusively for ascetics and ardent spiritual seekers. It is, in fact, a guide for individuals from all strata of society. While the Gita does present some of the highest spiritual wisdom that may be hard for an ordinary person to grasp at first contact, its teachings are not limited to those seeking renunciation and seclusion. The knowledge of the Gita was imparted to a warrior on the battlefield to lift him from his despondency and empower him to fulfill his bounden duty. It was not given out on the peaks of the Himalayas or in the depths of the forests. By the sheer context of its place of delivery, it is evident that the teachings of the Gita would most likely serve a dynamic human being actively engaged in the world.

In the fifth chapter of the Gita, Krishna clarifies that the householder's path is not only valid but often the most suited for most individuals aspiring for spiritual evolution. The teachings are not confined to those who withdraw from worldly responsibilities; instead, they illuminate how to bring the sacred into the ordinary and transform daily actions into acts of devotion. The wisdom of the Gita is universally applicable and, when turned to, positively impacts the lives of soldiers, professionals, workers, and individuals from all levels of society. It inspires us to infuse mundane tasks with meaning and purpose and make every moment a sacred opportunity for spiritual growth.

7. The Bhagavad Gita Promotes Casteism or Brahmanical Supremacy

The Bhagavad Gita has, unfortunately, faced false allegations of promoting casteism or Brahmanical supremacy. However, such accusations are far from the truth and stem from a lack of understanding of the fundamental principles of Advaita Vedanta. The vision of the Gita is oneness, which emphasizes that the wise perceive the same divine truth in all beings, irrespective of caste or creed.

Some prejudiced individuals selectively quote a verse from the fourth chapter of the Gita, where Krishna mentions creating the fourfold *varna* system. However, they conveniently omit the subsequent line, where Krishna clearly states that this classification is based on mental temperaments, not social hierarchy. The Gita aims to prescribe appropriate spiritual practices based on individual mental dispositions. It assures us that with sincere self-effort, anyone can evolve higher from where they presently are.

Furthermore, it is worth noting that Krishna himself, the divine teacher of the Gita, was not born into a Brahmin family, and according to the current social order, he belongs to the Other Backward Community (OBC) class. Similarly, *Maharishi* Vyasa, the compiler of the Gita, was the son of a fisherwoman. These examples highlight that the wisdom of the Gita does not condone or encourage caste-based supremacy. Instead, it emphatically promotes equality and unity for all of humanity. Taking random and incomplete phrases from within the text without connecting them to the context of preceding and ensuing verses spreads these misconstrued notions. Rest assured, as we steadily progress through the study of the Gita, its intended purpose as a unifying force will shine through.

8. The Bhagavad Gita is A Post-Retirement Spiritual Exercise

It is wrongly believed that the study of the Bhagavad Gita is best taken up only after retirement. This notion could not be further from the truth and does a disservice to humanity. The Gita is not just a philosophical treatise reserved for the twilight years of one's life, but a necessary manual for navigating life's very perplexing terrain.

As Swami Chinmayananda says, "Without a daily dose of spiritual (Bhagavad Gita) teachings, it is impossible to bear the onslaughts of human existence."

Imagine carrying a GPS device on a long journey but using it only in the final stretch. By doing so, we miss its invaluable guidance and assistance throughout the entire trip. Similarly, the Gita offers profound wisdom and insights that can enrich one's life from youth to old age. Delaying study until retirement means missing out on the immense benefits and solutions it provides for the various challenges we encounter throughout our lives. Befriending the Gita as a lifelong companion empowers us to make conscious choices, find purpose, and lead a fulfilling life from the very beginning of our journey. Let us not fall prey to this myth, but instead embrace the timeless teachings of the Gita and unlock its transformative power through every stage of life.

9. The Teachings of the Bhagavad Gita Contradict the Teachings of the Upanishads

Some readers of the Bhagavad Gita perceive a glaring contradiction between its teachings and those in the Upanishads.

When this misconception was presented to Swami Dayananda Sarasvati, he responded with wisdom, saying, '*Whenever you find yourself doubting that there is a discrepancy between the teachings of the Bhagavad Gita and those of the Upanishads, it is essential to question your own understanding of these scriptures rather than doubt their teachings.*'

In truth, there is no disparity between the Bhagavad Gita and the Upanishads; they convey the same profound message. As discussed earlier, the Gita is a more accessible version of the Upanishads, particularly for individuals immersed in the complexities of the world. It is the distilled essence of the Upanishads.

10. Possessing the Bhagavad Gita or Mahabharata in the Home Leads to Family Disputes

Because the Mahabharata is a chronicle of war and the Bhagavad Gita is a part of it, weak minds are plagued by this superstition that possessing or studying either would ignite family feuds and unrest within the household.

This belief is by far the most unreasonable belief anyone can hold onto. The very nature of the material world is conflict, and relationship disturbances exist with or without owning or studying any scripture of any faith, let alone the Bhagavad Gita.

Consider this: amidst the chaos of the monumental Mahabharata war, the teachings of the Bhagavad Gita were able to calm and provide clarity to an overwhelmingly distraught mind. If they could have such a dramatic impact in such a dire situation, imagine their power to resolve disputes within a household. The central message of the Bhagavad Gita emphasizes maintaining stability and a calm mind in all life situations, which one cannot provoke or be exasperated by.

Whether a home experiences conflicts or enjoys peace and harmony, the Mahabharata story serves as a reminder of how excessive egos can disrupt families. It highlights the destruction caused when feelings are prioritized over *Dharma* (what is to be done). Having the guidance of the Lord in the form of the Gita within our homes and hearts to illuminate our shortcomings and guide us away from our lower nature (the root cause of sorrow) is a blessing bestowed upon the fortunate few. When understood correctly, the teachings of the Bhagavad Gita hold the potential to help us avoid and resolve conflicts within and around us and lead us steadily toward Self-Realization.

We hope that through this exploration, we have successfully busted some of the prevalent myths surrounding the Bhagavad Gita. In a world where hearsay often shapes our perceptions, it is essential not to let unvalidated beliefs hinder our pursuit of Gita's profound wisdom. Let it be known that, over time, misconceptions can crystallize into accepted truths, a trap we must vigilantly avoid. Instead, approach the Gita with an open heart and an unbiased intellect and delve into its teachings with the intention of spiritual evolution and Self-realization. We must actively engage with, study, understand, practice, and experience its teachings firsthand to fully grasp its true value.

"Embrace the teachings of the Gita with an open heart and a discerning mind; from that confluence will flow the spirit of true understanding."

Bhagavad Gita's Influence on Eminent Personalities Across the World

The profound wisdom of the Bhagavad Gita has dramatically influenced the lives of prominent personalities worldwide, encouraging them to embrace noble ideals, lead with purpose, and make meaningful contributions to humanity. The Gita's positive impact on the lives of these significant historical figures is a testament to its universal appeal and timeless relevance.

Mahatma Gandhi: The Gita's emphasis on selfless service and righteous action resonated profoundly with Mahatma Gandhi, shaping his philosophy of non-violence and Satyagraha during India's struggle for independence. He often turned to the Gita for solace and inspiration in times of doubt and despair. [16]

Aldous Huxley: An English writer, Aldous Huxley, found the Gita to be a systematic and spiritually enriching treatise with enduring value not limited to India but applicable to all humanity. Its teachings profoundly influenced his perspective on life and spirituality. [17]

J. Robert Oppenheimer: The American physicist and director of the Manhattan Project, J. Robert Oppenheimer, discovered profound insights in the Gita, especially during the Trinity nuclear test, where he recalled verses from the scripture. [18]

Henry David Thoreau: The American philosopher and writer Henry David Thoreau was deeply moved by the Gita's majestic philosophy, considering it far superior to the ordinary literature of his time. Early morning reflections on its teachings ignited his imagination and philosophical thoughts. [19]

Hermann Graf Keyserling: A German philosopher, Hermann Graf Keyserling, considered the Bhagavad Gita one of the most beautiful works of literature in the world, admiring its profound depth and lofty wisdom. [20]

Ralph Waldo Emerson: Emerson, a prominent American essayist and poet, hailed Gita's wisdom as that of an empire, addressing profound questions and presenting an old intelligence that resonated with his philosophical musings. [21]

Wilhelm von Humboldt: The Gita deeply moved Wilhelm von Humboldt, who regarded it as the most beautiful and true philosophical song in any known tongue, with its wisdom touching the depths of human understanding. [22]

Bulent Ecevit: The former Turkish Prime Minister, Bulent Ecevit, found courage in Gita's teachings, inspiring him to act fearlessly against injustice while upholding moral righteousness. [23]

We have presented a cross-section of individuals from diverse backgrounds whose lives were illumined by the brilliance of the Bhagavad Gita. Beyond these illustrious figures, the Gita continues to influence today's artists, musicians, writers, and people, inspiring them to explore the depth of their inner selves and strive for a purposeful existence. We hope these citations will inspire aspiring students of the Gita to recognize its transformative power and potential. May they kindle and keep ablaze your curiosity to study the sacred verses of the Bhagavad Gita and experience its timeless wisdom firsthand.

"Down the ages, the Bhagavad Gita continues to inspire leaders, thinkers, and artists alike, showing us that its wisdom remains as relevant today as it was thousands of years ago."

Conclusion

The Bhagavad Gita is not just a sacred scripture to be blindly worshipped; neither is it merely a philosophical text to be casually read nor a scholarly analysis to be mastered. It is a clarion call to humanity to embark on an extraordinary inner pilgrimage that promises transformation on every level of the personality. It is a roadmap to navigate life's challenges, develop efficiency, surpass all limitations, clinch our true potential, find contentment, and evolve spiritually. An in-depth analysis of the Bhagavad Gita expands our understanding of human existence within the context of an otherwise incomprehensible cosmos.

Through this book, we present a distilled version of the traditional teachings of the Bhagavad Gita, as expounded by the most outstanding Advaita Vedanta teachers of the past and present, in a more relatable, relevant, and modern format than they have been before. We urge you to explore its timeless wisdom with an open and receptive mind. May the insights and solutions the Bhagavad Gita offers serve as motivation and solace through life's never-ending challenges. Together, let us delve into the profound depths of the Bhagavad Gita and unearth the precious gems of wisdom it holds for all who approach it with humility and devotion.

> *"May the Bhagavad Gita be our constant companion, illuminating our paths to prosperity, peace, joy, and wisdom."*

Gita Dhyanam

A Meditative Prelude

"The Gita Dhyanam is a devotional prelude to the symphony of spiritual wisdom that echoes through the Bhagavad Gita."

Dhyana Shlokas - The Sacred Bridge

Dhyana Shlokas have been an essential part of *Sanatana Dharma* for millennia, emphasizing the importance of the right intention and focus for one's spiritual quest. Like any invocation, which is a prayer chanted before any *sadhana* or spiritual practice to center oneself, the *Dhyana Shlokas* serves to connect the seeker's mind to the Divine before embarking on the paths of *Karma* (rituals), *Upasana* (meditation), or *Jnana* (study of scriptures).

What do the words *Dhyana Shloka* mean? *Dhyana* stems from the Sanskrit root (*Dhaatu)Dhi*, which pertains to perceiving, understanding, or contemplating. The suffix '*Ya*' is a common linguistic addition used to form nouns from root words, especially when indicating a specific state, action, or condition tied to the root. As a result, the derived term *Dhyanam* denotes deep, focused contemplation or attention.

Shloka springs from the root *Sru,* which means 'to hear.' *Shloka* is thus defined as what is heard or should be heard. But beyond its literal meaning, the characteristics of a *shloka* are intricately woven with the rhythm of language. It must adhere to a specific metric pattern to be termed a *Shloka*. Each *shloka* possesses a certain meter (*chhanda*), a defined number of lines, and a preset count of syllables in each line. The most prevalent of these meters is the *anushtubh*, already studied earlier, which elegantly frames its content within four lines, each containing eight syllables. While *shlokas* can be both rhymed and unrhymed, consistency is key if they bear rhymes. Features like alliteration, where consonant sounds echo at the beginnings of words, and assonance, the harmonious repetition of vowel sounds within words, enhance the beauty of these verses. The vivid imagery that paints evocative pictures in the reader's mind accentuates the effect of these *shlokas*.

Where did *shlokas* originate? Legend has it that the first *shloka* sprang from the sadness (*shoka*) of Sage Valmiki, the revered author of the Ramayana. Upon witnessing a hunter shoot one of a pair of loving birds, his emotions identified with the desolation of the surviving bird. This surge of emotion birthed the very first *shloka*. Valmiki then sculpted the entirety of the Ramayana in the form of these metrically patterned *shlokas*, giving the epic its rhythmic cadence. This pattern of *shlokas* became the hallmark of our literary legacy and bestowed him with the title *Adikavi,* or the first poet.

Dhyana Shlokas are thus aptly translated as 'meditative verses.' When reverentially chanted or deeply reflected upon, they connect the seeker to profound spiritual sentiment.

Dhyana Shlokas has historical roots buried deep within the Indian spiritual tradition. These verses preface various texts, including the *Rudram* (a Vedic chant paying homage to Lord Shiva) and *Sahasranamas* (recitation of a thousand names in remembrance and glorification of different deities). The *Dhyana Shlokas* have been passed down through generations of spiritual masters as an essential component in directing the spiritual journey.

Significance of Dhyana Shlokas

Let us explore how the timeless relevance of the *Dhyana Shlokas* continues to benefit spiritual seekers.

Setting the Right Mood and Mindset

The *Dhyana Shlokas* serve as a prelude to spiritual engagement, harmonizing the inner ambiance of the seeker. Their melodic recitation calms the wandering mind, preparing a serene canvas for the spiritual artwork ahead. It is akin to tuning an instrument before a grand performance, ensuring the mind is perfectly pitched for divine resonance.

Tool for Visualization

The *Dhyana Shlokas* could be likened to a tool that helps form a tangible connection with the chosen deity. For example, the *Dhyana Shloka* of *Vishnu Sahasranama* facilitates a link to Divinity worshipped as Lord Vishnu. Similarly, the *Gita Dhyanam*, which translates as Meditation on the Gita, helps the seeker invoke *Bhagavan* Shri Krishna's grace and deeply connect to the wisdom emanating from His enlightening words in the Bhagavad Gita.

Invoking Divine Presence

The *Dhyana Shlokas* bridge the gap between finite human intellect and infinite Divine wisdom. Contemplating or chanting these verses connects the seeker's mind to the Higher and infuses one's spiritual practice with the comforting light of Divine guidance. They make way, as it were, for a deeper, more harmonious alignment with spiritual truths.

Enhancing Devotion

Spirituality, at its core, thrives on devotion. The profound essence of the *Dhyana Shlokas* fans the flames of this innate devotion. By chanting these verses with pure devotion and single-pointed focus, we create a sacred space within, ready to receive the teachings and grace of the Divine. The depth of their meaning stirs the soul, catalyzing a deepened reverence and commitment that transforms each spiritual endeavor into a heartfelt communion.

Aiding Concentration

Life is riddled with endless distractions, and concentration often remains elusive. *Dhyana Shlokas* serve as a sanctified anchor by drawing the scattered energies of the mind and channeling them into a singular stream of focused awareness. By chanting these verses, one tunes into the articulatory and intonational power of the words, which sets the stage for a meditative state that is both profound and effective.

Transcending the Ego

The ego often veils our true essence. The *Dhyana Shlokas*, like mirrors, reflect the impermanence of existence. They gently nudge the seeker into an awareness transcending the ego to realize a reality beyond the little self.

Protection and Purification

Sanctity of mind is paramount in the quest for spiritual enlightenment. The *Dhyana Shlokas* stand as vigilant sentinels, safeguarding our thoughts. With each recitation, they ward off negativity, purify our minds, and ensure a seamless journey ahead.

Generating Positive Vibrations

The power of language is undeniable, and Sanskrit, often hailed as the sacred language of spirituality is its own testament. When one chants the *Dhyana Shlokas* in this ancient tongue, there unfurls a cascade of positive vibrations. The rhythm and cadence of the verses create a pitch-perfect harmony that stirs a sense of well-being from deep within.

Among the myriad spiritual practices within *Sanatana Dharma,* the *Dhyana Shlokas* distinguishingly harmonize the seeker's heart and mind.

Their timeless resonance underscores our inherent bond to the Divine and draws us closer to our spiritual essence. With reverential recitation of these verses, we embark on a sacred journey of gratitude for age-old traditions toward eternal wisdom and spiritual enlightenment.

The Beauty and Wisdom of Gita Dhyanam

The *Dhyana Shlokas* that preface the Bhagavad Gita are collectively called the *Gita Dhyanam*. The *Gita Dhyanam* is the very foundation upon which the temple of the Bhagavad Gita is built. It is a sequence of nine verses traditionally recited or chanted before commencing the study of the Gita. This purposeful ritualistic beginning, especially prevalent in the Advaita Vedanta tradition, sensitizes the mind and clarifies the intellect, preparing us for the profound spiritual insights that follow.

The Bhagavad Gita is part of the Mahabharata's vast narrative. However, the Gita Dhyanam is a unique treasure. It connects deeply with the Gita's teachings but also stands as a source of wisdom on its own. The authorship of these verses is commonly attributed to Madhusudana Sarasvati, though not conclusively verified. He lived from around 1540 CE to 1640 CE. He was an ardent devotee of *Bhagavan* Shri Krishna and a revered figure in the *Advaita Vedanta* lineage.

One of the charming features of *Gita Dhyanam* is its portrayal of the Bhagavad Gita as a devoted mother, always protecting her children. This powerful imagery reflects the nurturing and compassionate teachings that offer solace and wisdom, much like what is found in a mother's unconditional love.

The *Dhyana Shlokas* pay homage to Vyasa, the great sage who compiled these life-transforming teachings within the Mahabharata epic. This gesture acknowledges the vital bridge he built to connect humanity with the divine knowledge enshrined in these texts.

The *Dhyana Shlokas* also offer salutations to the Universal Teacher, *Bhagavan* Shri Krishna. They celebrate His role in imparting the highest and noblest teachings to humanity, highlighting the importance of skilled teachers in our lives who help us navigate our spiritual journey effectively.

The *Gita Dhyanam* distinctly defines the much-debated relationship between the Bhagavad Gita and the Upanishads. It portrays the Gita as capturing the essence of Upanishadic wisdom, refined and presented in a more lucid format. This connection validates the authenticity and universality of the Bhagavad Gita and its perfect alignment with the core vision of *Sanatana Dharma*.

By emphasizing the importance of Divine grace in human lives, the *Gita Dhyanam* encourages us to recognize that individual effort must be backed by faith in a higher power. This powerful combination of *prayatna* (self-effort) and *shraddha* (persevering faith) grounds us in our spiritual Reality as we engage in worldly transactions with a spirit of humility and deep devotion.

The *Gita Dhyanam* most accurately summarizes the Mahabharata saga, within which the Bhagavad Gita is embedded, highlighting its relevance in *Kaliyuga* (current age). It exalts the Mahabharata as a monumental source of inspiration that continues to guide humanity through life's intersecting pathways.

Finally, the verses offer their obeisance to the fundamental form of Divinity - Absolute Truth, Existence, and Consciousness. This act transcends personal and sectarian beliefs and aligns the seeker with the foundational principles of existence.

The *Gita Dhyanam* is a sacred gateway that takes us straight into the heart of the Bhagavad Gita. Its rich symbolism, thoughtful salutations, and profound insights set the stage for unveiling the intimate dialogue between the Lord of Yoga, *Bhagavan* Shri Krishna, and the supreme archer Arjuna, assuring us of a genuinely transformative and illuminating experience. The Gita Dhyanam is a cascade of devotion that gushes to merge into an ocean of wisdom, making it a befitting curtain-raiser to the timeless teachings of the Bhagavad Gita.

Contemplation upon the Gita Dhyana Shlokas: Verse-by-Verse Analysis

Shloka 1: Salutations to Gita: The Nurturing Mother

ॐ पार्थाय प्रतिबोधितां भगवता नारायणेन स्वयं
व्यासेन ग्रथितां पुराणमुनिना मध्ये महाभारतम्।
अद्वैतामृतवर्षिणीं भगवतीम् अष्टादशाध्यायिनीं
अम्ब त्वाम् अनुसन्दधामि भगवद्गीते भवद्वेषिणीम्॥ (1)

ōṁ pārthāya pratibōdhitāṁ bhagavatā nārāyaṇēna svayaṁ
vyāsēna grathitāṁ purāṇamuninā madhyē mahābhāratam|
advaitāmṛtavarṣiṇīṁ bhagavatīm aṣṭādaśādhyāyinīṁ
amba tvām anusandadhāmi bhagavadgītē bhavadvēṣiṇīm|| (1)

"OM. O Mother Bhagavad Gita! You were imparted by the divine Lord Narayana Himself to enlighten Arjuna. Faithfully compiled by the ancient sage Vyasa, you find your esteemed place in the heart of the Mahabharata. Spread across 18 chapters, you shower the nectar of Advaita, standing as a beacon against life's adversities. Repeatedly, I turn to you, the very essence that dispels worldly dilemmas" (*Gita Dhyanam: 1*)

The Divine Invocation: An Auspicious Beginning

Within *Sanatana Dharma*, all auspicious beginnings are initiated with the sacred chant of OM. Besides being an age-old tradition, this practice holds great spiritual significance.

The syllable OM is a profound encapsulation of Universal Intelligence or *Ishavara.*

तस्य वाचकः प्रणवः ॥२७॥ Yoga Sutra (1:27)

OM (Pranava) is the word denoting Ishvara (Universal Intelligence).

Therefore, commencing the *Gita Dhyanam* by chanting the OM is not just an arbitrary convention but an indication of the deeply spiritual journey one is about to undertake. It sets the tone by instantaneously rendering the mind entirely receptive to the wisdom that is to unfold.

Gita: The Compassionate Mother

A remarkable facet of this *shloka* is its portrayal of the Bhagavad Gita as a mother. Apart from being presented in the form of the most exquisite poetry, this verse is a flawless reflection of how the Gita functions in the life of a seeker. Just as a mother nourishes, guides, protects, and showers unconditional love upon her child, the Gita assures spiritual sustenance.

Like a mother who births a child into the world, the Gita births a holistically sound personality out of the seeker. Just as the mother is the physical womb of a human being, the Gita is considered the spiritual womb. A biological umbilical cord keeps the child connected with the mother through gestation. Similarly, the wisdom of the Gita is an invisible spiritual umbilical cord that holds the seeker connected with the Supreme throughout the mortal sojourn. When children face worldly atrocities, they seek comfort in the mother's lap. Similarly, whenever a seeker faces untoward challenges in life, they seek solace in the uplifting wisdom of Mother Gita.

This analogy beautifully illustrates Gita's ability to uncover the root cause of various problems, ease anxiety, and offer pragmatic solutions to resolve conflicts while continually showering the seeker with love, thus highlighting its motherly role in nurturing one's spiritual growth. It connects, as it were, the heart of the seeker to the heart of the Gita, as a child to its mother.

Ancient seekers of bygone eras were not the only ones who undeniably experienced the maternal warmth of the Bhagavad Gita. Mahatma Gandhi, one of the finest human beings the world has ever witnessed, revered the Bhagavad Gita as his "eternal mother." He felt the Gita's embrace more comforting than his earthly mother's, especially during the darkest hours of his life. No other scripture influenced Gandhi as the Gita did. He once said, *"When doubts haunt me, when disappointments stare me in the face, and when I see not one ray of light on the horizon, I run to the Bhagavad Gita and find a verse to comfort me, and I immediately begin to smile in the midst of overwhelming sorrow."* Such was the magnanimous influence of the Bhagavad Gita in his life. It was far more than a scripture for him. The Gita was his mother and guide, and she never failed him [24].

The Trinity: Student, Teacher, and Compiler

The opening *shloka* eloquently brings into the spotlight three pivotal figures of the Bhagavad Gita, starting with Arjuna, a stereotypical student grappling with a personal crisis. His struggles are emblematic of the human condition, teetering between personal emotion and *Dharma*. Within Arjuna's incapacitating predicament, we recognize our own.

This heartwarming *shloka* lauds Krishna as the Divine Teacher. It poeticizes how Krishna, besides providing great solace, offers transformative spiritual insights, grounding Arjuna (and all of humanity) in the life principles of *Dharma*, duty, and the nature of existence.

The *shloka* also reverently addresses Krishna as Narayana. Composed of two words, *Nara* (human) and *Ayana* (shelter or destination), Narayana symbolizes humanity's ultimate refuge or destination.

By glorifying Krishna as Narayana, the *shloka* pays homage to His Divine nature and emphasizes that the teachings of the Gita are the ultimate guiding principles for human life. The fact that these teachings emanate from Lord Narayana Himself validates their authenticity, assuring us they are unblemished by human interference.

The *shloka* goes on to bestow adorations upon Sage Vyasa, the chronicler, who ensured that these teachings reach future generations. By placing the Bhagavad Gita amidst the grand narrative of the Mahabharata, Vyasa elevated its significance, intertwining its teachings with the broader lessons of the epic.

The Essence of Advaita

The Bhagavad Gita is a reservoir of wisdom and a guide for life. At its core lies the doctrine of *Advaita*, the non-dual nature of existence. By likening the teachings of the Bhagavad Gita to the "nectar of *Advaita*," the *shloka* iterates the transformative power of *Advaita Vedanta's* quintessential vision of Oneness. Like nectar, which offers immortality, a root understanding of *Advaita* teachings offers spiritual immortality by revealing the true nature of oneself.

The Structure and Impact of Gita

And finally, the *shloka* touches upon the very structure of the Gita. Its 701 verses, spread across 18 chapters, are a keen examination of the comprehensive nature of its teachings. Every *shloka*, every chapter, is a step toward the supreme goal of life. The Bhagavad Gita is an effective tool that helps us transcend our limitations and realize our true nature.

Summary

This *shloka* exemplifies how the Gita is a wise counsel, without discrimination, for all those struggling with complex problems and consistently provides systematic, scientific, and logical solutions to tackle and rise above them. It highlights to every sincere seeker the Gita's assurance of a transformative journey that will take them from being a victim in life to a victor in all circumstances.

This captivating first *shloka* of the *Gita Dhyanam* is a microcosm of the essence, significance, and impact of the entire Bhagavad Gita. It introduces us to the Gita's timeless wisdom, universality, and enduring relevance in guiding humanity toward truth and enlightenment.

"As a mother's touch softens life's blows, so the Bhagavad Gita shelters us beneath the grace of the comforting warmth of its infinite wisdom."

Shloka 2: Salutations to Vyasa: Illuminator of Ancient Wisdom

नमोऽस्तुते व्यास विशालबुद्धे फुल्लारविन्दायतपत्रनेत्र |
येन त्वया भारत तैलपूर्णः प्रज्वालितो ज्ञानमयः प्रदीपः|| (2)

namō'stutē vyāsa viśālabuddhē phullāravindāyatapatranētra |
yēna tvayā bhārata tailapūrṇaḥ prajvālitō jñānamayaḥ pradīpaḥ|| (2)

"Salutations to thee, O Vyasa, of vast intellect, whose eyes resemble the petals of a fully bloomed lotus. You are the one who kindled the lamp of knowledge, filled with the oil of the Mahabharata." (*Gita Dhyanam: 2*)

The primary focus of the second *shloka* of the *Gita Dhyanam* is its acknowledgment and deep reverence for Sage Vyasa, the very bedrock of ancient Indian spiritual literature. The verse worshipfully glorifies this literary genius with soulful descriptions of his sheer beauty and the vastness of his intellect.

Vyasa's Illustrious Intellect

Vyasa, whose birth name was Krishna Dwaipayana, was born to sage Parashara and a fisherwoman, Satyavati, on an island in the river Yamuna. The name *Vyasa* translates as 'the dark-complexioned one born on an island.' Yet, despite his modest origins, he became a revered sage of unparalleled knowledge through sheer perseverance and self-effort.

The honorific title Veda Vyasa, which means 'the Compiler of the Vedas,' is itself an ode to his immense contributions. The Vedas, in their original form, were a vast reservoir of knowledge without logical compartmentalization. Recognizing the need for a systematic approach, Vyasa meticulously compiled and categorized the teachings of India's ancient sages into the four well-known Vedas: *Rig, Yajus, Sama,* and *Atharva.* Furthermore, he brilliantly organized the contents of each Veda into four distinct sections: *Mantra, Brahmana, Aranyaka,* and *Upanishads.*

Compiling and classifying such an extensive body of knowledge was no ordinary feat. It required a thorough understanding of the subject matter and keen foresight to envision the needs of future generations. Vyasa's monumental contribution became the foundation for disseminating the teachings of *Sanatana Dharma.*

Vyasa's intellectual and spiritual prowess was not limited to the Vedas. He further enriched the tapestry of Vedic teachings with his compositions of the epic Mahabharata and 18 Puranas. These texts, particularly the Mahabharata, are a testament to Vyasa's profound understanding of *Dharma* and the nature of the human psyche. The entire spectrum of human emotions can be identified within the exhaustive script of the Mahabharata. Through his intelligent portrayal of diverse characters, be they kings, queens, sages, warriors, or the common folk, he painted a complete picture of the myriad shades of human nature and the society of the time.

There is a saying, *VYASOCHISTAM JAGAT SARVAM,* which means there is no aspect of humanity's past, present, or future condition that Vyasa has not touched upon. This statement is not an exaggeration, especially considering the magnitude of the Mahabharata. Holding the distinction of being the longest epic poem known to humankind, the Mahabharata encompasses approximately 1.8 million words! Given that the Mahabharata is about ten times the combined length of the Iliad and the Odyssey, Vyasa's works have no parallel in-depth, diversity, or philosophical grandeur within the context of world literature.

Vyasa's expansive intellect, vividly described by the term *viśālabuddhe* in the *shloka*, truly epitomizes the profundity of his knowledge. His insightful exploration of literature, human nature, and spirituality is evident through every word of his various compositions. Each of his exceptional works is a testimony to his deep contemplation of life.

This homage to Vyasa, so beautifully offered right at the beginning of the *Gita Dhyanam*, firmly establishes the sage's towering stature and prepares the reader for the immensity of wisdom and insight that follows in the Bhagavad Gita.

Eyes Bearing Unblemished Clarity

Vyasa's vision is elucidated with a poetic analogy, *phullāravindāyatapatranetra* - which means one graced with eyes as splendid as the petals of a fully bloomed lotus. In traditional Indian literature, clear, radiant eyes bear greater symbolism than mere aesthetic appreciation. They denote clarity of vision. They reflect the purity of the mind and the depth of understanding. Such an enlightened vision allows one to perceive the essence of existence unfettered by illusions and misconceptions.

The significance of clarity of vision cannot be overstated. Just as a clear mirror reflects images without distortion, the sages' clear visions accurately perceive truths. It allows them to rise above mere appearances, discern subtler truths, and guide others with the wisdom derived from such lucid insights.

The Lamp of Profound Wisdom

The *shloka* further decorates Vyasa with a majestic title: *prajjvālitaḥ jñānamaya pradīpaḥ—the* one who ignited the radiant lamp of knowledge. The lamp here is a potent symbol. Just as the light of a lamp drives away the darkness, the knowledge imparted by Vyasa disperses the shadows of ignorance.

Beautifully described as *bhāratatailapūrṇa,* the fuel for this lamp of wisdom is most accurately said to be none other than the Mahabharata. Often revered as the fifth Veda, the Mahabharata is not just an epic; it is a canvas upon which the elaborate compositions of Vedic knowledge are brought to life with historical tales of the land, thus asserting the age-old maxim, *Vedokhilo Dharma Moolam,* meaning, "The root of Veda is the *Dharma.*" Just as roots give life to a tree, the vision and precepts of *Dharma* are enlivened through the mesmerizing narratives of the Mahabharata.

Vyasa's scriptural masterpiece revolves around the central theme of *Dharma.* He captivates seekers by presenting philosophical truths cleverly intertwined with tales of valor, ethics, and morality. This *shloka* beautifully captures the symbiotic relationship between knowledge and its applicability. The lamp (knowledge) derives its sustenance from the oil (Mahabharata), and in tandem, they spread light, dispelling the gloom of unawareness and enlightening countless beings.

And so do the potent works of Vyasa, which illuminate the past and continue to light the path of future generations. Moreover, in today's globally connected and rapidly evolving world, Vyasa's timeless writings provide guidance and solace through life's complexities, revealing their ongoing relevance.

Summary

The second *shloka* of the *Gita Dhyanam* is a prayerful tribute to the revered Sage Vyasa, a luminary of ancient Indian spiritual literature. With an intellect as vast as the horizons, Vyasa is poetically described as possessing eyes as radiant and clear as the petals of a blossoming lotus, symbolizing his profound clarity of vision and exceptional insight into the nature of existence. Beyond being the epitome of embodied knowledge, Vyasa's crowning achievement lies in illuminating the path of wisdom for countless seekers. He masterfully kindled the radiant lamp of knowledge, using the captivating tales of the Mahabharata as its sustaining oil. He continues to guide innumerable generations through this luminous flame of wisdom and understanding.

"Vyasa's intellect as boundless as the sky and the clarity of his vision kindled the lamp of knowledge by using the Mahabharata as its fuel, to light the way for generations."

Shloka 3: Salutations to Krishna: Harmony Amid Life's Challenges

प्रपन्नपारिजाताय तोत्रवेत्रैकपाणये |
ज्ञानमुद्राय कृष्णाय गीतामृतदुहे नमः || (3)

prapannapārijātāya tōtravētraikapāṇayē |
jñānamudrāya kṛṣṇāya gītāmṛtaduhē namaḥ || (3)

"My salutations to Krishna, the wish-fulfilling tree for those who surrender to him. He holds a whip in one hand and the Jnana Mudra (hand gesture denoting wisdom) in the other. He is the one who extracts the essence of the Gita." *(Gita Dhyanam: 3)*

The third *shloka* of *Gita Dhyanam* celebrates the Divine form of Krishna in all its glory and venerates His immortal teachings in the form of the Bhagavad Gita.

Salutations to the Wondrous Krishna

The *shloka* commences with salutations to *Bhagavan* Shri Krishna. This fervent adulation is not a mere mechanical prostration before a deity but a deep reverence for the unfathomable depths of Krishna's magnificence.

Granter of Legitimate Desires: The Wish-fulfilling Tree

The *shloka* hails Krishna as *Prapannapārijātāya,* likening him to the mythological *Parijata,* or wish-fulfilling tree that grants all wishes, creatively iterating that those who surrender to Krishna's teachings align with the cosmic order. In this complete alignment, all efforts naturally find fruition. It accentuates the symbiotic relationship between mortal wishes and Divine Will, in which, ironically, surrendering one's ego and desires to the Divine fulfills those desires.

The Charismatic Charioteer: Mastery over Body and Mind

In the Mahabharata war, Krishna stands as Arjuna's charioteer, holding a whip in one hand. This portrayal epitomizes Krishna's humility despite being the Lord of the Universe. The horses symbolize our senses, the reins represent our mind, and Krishna's whip represents control over the instinctual senses. In a spirit of total surrender to Krishna, one can acquire the same mastery as Him by purposefully directing the mind and senses as He does reins and horses.

The Emblem of Ultimate Knowledge: *Jnana Mudra*

Krishna's one hand holding a *Jnana Mudra* is an intriguing sight. This extraordinary imagery entirely captures the essence of Krishna's teachings in the Bhagavad Gita by seamlessly intertwining the material and the spiritual facets of human life.

Mudras, in the yogic spiritual tradition, are not mere hand gestures. They are powerful symbolic configurations, representing subtler truths and insights. They serve as conduits, channeling cosmic order into our very being. Each *mudra* carries a distinct spiritual message and has specific significance in the meditative process. *Jnana Mudra*, among these, stands out with its emphasis on love for knowledge.

Pause and bring your hand into the *Jnana Mudra* for a moment. In this gesture, the middle, ring, and little fingers stand erect, aloof from the index finger, which elegantly curves to meet the mighty thumb, forming a seamless circle. This alignment illuminates the state toward self-realization.

The index finger, often dubbed the 'accusing finger,' symbolizes the individual self or the ego. It is how we often distinguish and separate ourselves from the universe. I versus you. Us versus them. In its natural unbended state, the index finger joins with the other three fingers, highlighting our mundane identification with our body, mind, and intellect. However, when consciously pulled away, the journey to Self-Realization begins, as it were. This deliberate separation asserts that our real essence is not defined by or limited to our body, mind, or intellect. These are *anatma* (not Self). Mistaking them for our true nature, *atma* (Self), is a fundamental human misperception.

As Swami Chinmayananda succinctly puts it, "The non-apprehension of Reality causes misapprehension of Reality." Not understanding our true Self as Pure Consciousness, we take the body, mind, and intellect as ourselves (*adhyasa*). [25]

The thumb in this arrangement denotes the limitless *Brahman*, the ultimate Reality or Universal Consciousness. It stands apart, unattached, much like *Brahman*, though enlivening it all, remains detached from worldly manifestations. Without the thumb, the hand loses its functional capabilities. Similarly, without *Brahman*, our individual existence cannot assert itself; our body, mind, and intellect cannot function. The joining of the thumb and index finger to create a circle personifies the union of the individual self and Universal Consciousness. The circle, having no beginning or end, emphasizes the concept of infinity, suggesting that we will recognize our limitless nature when we attain spiritual knowledge.

As Swami Ranganathananda teaches [26], the very act of forming the *Jnana Mudra* generates the intent to seek knowledge and move from the mundane to the profound. Our unique human ability to bring the thumb and forefinger together illustrates our evolutionary advantage to seek, grasp, and internalize knowledge. As Swami Ji beautifully elucidates, the opposing thumb and forefinger are not just a biological design but a reflection of humanity's incessant thirst for knowledge. By holding the *Jnana Mudra*, we are not just positioning our fingers in a certain way but also setting into motion a millennia-old tradition that venerates the quest for knowledge and Self-Realization.

Balancing Action and Inner Serenity

This enigmatic portrayal of Krishna with a whip in one hand and holding a *Jnana Mudra* with the other baffles many. Rest assured; this deliberate contradiction expounds a profound vision that is the very heart of the Bhagavad Gita.

The whip represents diligence, hard work, and active engagement in the material world. It stresses the necessity of performing one's duty, or *Dharma*, with dedication and vigor. The world demands action, and Krishna, the charioteer in this setting, emphatically asserts the importance of rightful action, or *karma*.

On the other hand, the *Jnana Mudra* exemplifies wisdom, introspection, and inner peace. It rouses us to cultivate a reflective and tranquil mind well-established in knowledge. While the whip drives our attention outward, the *Jnana Mudra* lures us inward to a realm beyond mere action—one of understanding, contemplation, and spiritual enlightenment.

Together, the whip and *Jnana Mudra* demonstrate the necessity of a balanced lifestyle. These potent symbols herald dynamic action in the world, sustained by introspective wisdom. Such a perfect equilibrium orchestrates a harmonious symphony between the outer and inner worlds, the active and the reflective, and the temporal and the eternal. Krishna champions this game-changing lifestyle that counterbalances diligent work and inner serenity throughout the Bhagavad Gita. He offers humanity a comprehensive approach to living a perfect life blessed with success and peace, which is especially relevant in today's increasingly tumultuous world.

Gita: The Elixir of Immortal Wisdom

This *shloka* likens the Gita to the nectar of immortality, a comparison deeply embedded in our cultural and spiritual psyche.

As per mythological tales, *Amritam,* or "Divine Nectar," bestows immortality upon its recipients. Everybody, without exception, consciously or unconsciously desires an escape from death, as it spells an end to our transient existence. The Gita offers a similar elixir, not in a tangible form but as profound teachings that challenge our understanding of mortality. It shifts our identification with the ephemeral body, mind, and intellect to align it more with our true essence, which is a part of the boundless Universal Consciousness. Just as Divine Nectar is known to give eternal life, the wisdom of the Gita blesses us with a vision of the Self beyond birth and death. It introduces us to the truth of our own immortality, which is interwoven with the eternity of universal existence itself.

But where does this potent nectar ooze from? As touched upon earlier, the essence of the Gita is derived from the revered Upanishads, ancient scriptures that carry the crux of Vedic wisdom. The *shloka* likens all the Upanishads to a cow and the Divine teachings of the Gita to milk, the nourishing, life-giving essence distilled from vast knowledge. *Bhagavan* Shri Krishna, the cowherd boy, milks this nectar for the world. We offer our humble salutations to the distiller of this otherwise impenetrable wisdom.

Summary

Shloka 3 reverently salutes Krishna by employing rich analogies to convey the magnanimity of his Divine essence. Krishna is likened to the Parijata tree, known to grant the wishes of its beholders, emphasizing His role as the benevolent fulfiller of his devotees' desires. His two hands symbolize life's duality: one gripping a whip, emblematic of His mastery over circumstances, and the other gracefully formed into the *Jnana Mudra*, signifying an enduring devotion to knowledge. With boundless love and wisdom, Krishna milked the teachings of the Gita to guide humanity away from suffering and toward liberation.

"Holding a whip in one hand to tackle life's trials and a Jnana Mudra in the other to remain anchored in infinite wisdom, Krishna carries every sincere seeker out of turmoil into freedom."

Shloka 4: Echoes of Eternity: Gita as the Essence of the Upanishads

सर्वोपनिषदो गावः दोग्धा गोपालनन्दनः |
पार्थो वत्सः सुधीर्भोक्ता दुग्धं गीतामृतं महत् || (4)

sarvōpaniṣadō gāvaḥ dōgdhā gōpālanandanaḥ |
pārthō vatsaḥ sudhīrbhōktā dugdhaṁ gītāmṛtaṁ mahat | (4)

All Upanishads are likened to the cow; Krishna, the delight of the cowherds, is the milker; Arjuna, the eager calf; Those of discerning intellect and pure mind are the beneficiaries; And the invaluable, timeless nectar being drawn is the profound wisdom of the Gita *(Gita Dhyana Shloka: 4).*

Poetically declaring the Gita as the essence of all Upanishads, this *shloka* assures us that though the message of the Gita echoes through Krishna's voice and Arjuna's questions within the context of a mighty battle, it mirrors the timeless wisdom of the Upanishads. Therefore, the Bhagavad Gita and the Upanishads are fundamentally inseparable.

The Spiritual Cow: Upanishads, the Fountain of Knowledge

The Vedas, the most revered scriptures in *Sanatana Dharma*, have guided seekers on their path for millennia. The Upanishads make up the end portion of every Veda and hold the core scriptural tenets revealing the mysteries of our true nature. When we talk of Vedanta, we refer to the study of the Upanishads.

This *shloka* likens the Upanishads to a cow (*sarvōpaniṣadō gāvaḥ*), which is considered as an embodiment of service, sacrifice, prosperity, and purity in India. It explains that if the Upanishads are the cow, the cow's most precious gift, the milk, is the Bhagavad Gita. Thus, the Gita is the nourishing essence drawn from the Upanishads, distilled in a manner that humanity can readily absorb and thrive upon.

The Divine Milkman: Krishna's Gift of Gita

Krishna, fondly referred to as *Gopala Nandana* or the joy of the cowherds, plays the vital role of extracting the precious milk of the

Gita from the Upanishads (*dōgdhā*). While commonly defining '*go*' as cow in Sanskrit, '*go*' also denotes the Vedas. Here, Krishna is glorified not merely as the extractor of the essence of the Vedas but as the one who infuses life into its teachings. By rendering these complex Vedic teachings lucid enough for every intellect to grasp, He ensures their timeless essence remains intact and transferable down the ages.

Arjuna: The Catalyst Calf

It is a commonly observed fact that the presence of a calf induces the cow to yield milk, just as a mother is seen to telepathically lactate around her hungry newborn baby. In this allegory, Arjuna represents the calf (*pārthō vatsaḥ*). His insurmountable existential crisis on the battlefield of Kurukshetra symbolizes the stimulant that invoked the wisdom of the Gita from Krishna.

The Noble Beneficiaries: Humanity's Inheritance

Besides nourishing her famished calf, the cow's milk nourishes entire communities. Similarly, while the Bhagavad Gita was immediately meant for Arjuna, it extends beyond him to all of humanity, making his dilemmas and the teachings he received a universal template.

Bhagavad Gita sustains all pure-hearted and earnest seekers along their life journey. Its timeless relevance ensures a continual source of guidance for all of humankind.

Amrita: The Elixir of Life

The Gita's teachings likened to the nectar of immortality—*Amrita*, promise holistic well-being and direct us toward the zenith of life's potentialities. As its name suggests, the Gita offers sustenance and eternal happiness to those who imbibe its wisdom.

Summary

Shloka 4 glorifies the Bhagavad Gita as the essence of the Upanishads. It likens the Upanishads to a sacred cow and the Gita to its spiritually nourishing milk. Arjuna symbolizes the calf that prompts the release of wisdom from Krishna the Divine milkman. This wondrous analogy asserts the Gita's deep Vedic roots while emphasizing its enduring relevance for all seekers.

"Krishna distilled the essence of the Upanishads into the Bhagavad Gita for humanity. May we embrace it, internalize it, and secure our life's journey."

Shloka 5: Radiance of Krishna: The Universal Luminary

वसुदेवसुतं देवं कंसचाणूरमर्दनम् |
देवकीपरमानन्दं कृष्णं वन्दे जगद्गुरुम् || (5)

vasudēvasutaṁ dēvaṁ kaṁsacāṇūramardanam |
dēvakīparamānandaṁ kṛṣṇaṁ vandē jagadgurum || (5)

"I bow to Krishna, the universal teacher and Divine Lord, The son of Vasudeva, the vanquisher of Kamsa and Chanura, And the supreme delight of his mother, Devaki" *(Gita Dhyana Shloka 5)*

This *shloka* artistically weaves together the multifaceted splendor of Krishna by exalting Him as a universal guide, a vanquisher of evil, a champion of righteousness, and the perennial source of joy.

The Timeless Teacher: Krishna as *Jagad-Guru*

Krishna's embodied wisdom that breaks through time, geographical, and cultural barriers rightly earns Him the title *Jagad-Guru* or universal teacher. To be revered as a universal teacher, one's teachings must be globally relevant, far-reaching, and all-inclusive, transcending the bounds of time and context. Notably, Krishna's teachings appeal even to those of different faiths, who may not necessarily recognize him as a Divine incarnation.

That the imparted wisdom surpasses the teacher's identity is an irrefutable testimony to its universality. When the teachings rise above the stature of the teacher, the teacher is hailed as *Jagad-guru*. Today, many walk around with this self-ordained title, yet rare few genuinely embody it. Krishna's teachings in the Gita, which primarily address humanity's core dilemmas and point toward Self-Realization, remain ever pertinent.

Vanquisher of the Vicious: Krishna's Triumph over *Adharma*

This *shloka* reminds us of Krishna's victory over the demons Kamsa and Chanura (*kaṁsacāṇūramardanam*). But to see this as a mere historical or mythological event would be to miss its profound symbolic significance. These enemies exemplify the rampant evils and disorders that plague society. Krishna's conquest over them emphasizes the pivotal role of the righteous in upholding *Dharma* by resisting and eliminating forces of *adharma*. Puranic or ancient scriptural tales of Krishna and other deities defeating various asuras are allegorical narratives. These demons symbolize our own inner terrors, the *adharmic* or lower negative tendencies with which we constantly grapple. By invoking the grace of Divine knowledge, symbolized here by Krishna's *Sudarshana Chakra* (the discus that bestows the right vision), we, too, can defeat and overcome these internal foes.

The Wellspring of Joy: Krishna, the Giver of Happiness

Krishna was born to Vasudeva and was the wondrous delight of His mother, Devaki. However, these familial ties did not define the radius of his love and affection. He was a mine of happiness that effortlessly magnetized all hearts toward him. His presence, actions, and teachings offered tremendous peace and contentment to everyone around Him. The name Krishna itself is synonymous with attraction (*karshati*) - "He who draws all toward him."

Aren't we all, without exception, attracted to what brings us joy? In his Divine essence, Krishna is the very source of contentment, embodying and radiating happiness in its purest form, naturally making him the focal point of idolization for countless seekers along their spiritual journey.

Summary

As *Jagad-Guru*, Krishna's teachings are not confined to a particular age or group; they flawlessly synchronize with timeless truths that remain relevant for all individuals across epochs.

His role is not limited to imparting wisdom; he actively restores righteousness. By vanquishing demons like Kamsa and Chanura, He declares his firm commitment to eradicate evil tendencies and societal wrongdoing.

Krishna, the son of Vasudeva and the precious delight of Devaki, is revered as a universal symbol of love and wisdom. No doubt, He was the joy and happiness of His family. But up to this day, His compassionate aura touches and blesses the lives of all who approach Him with faith and devotion.

"Krishna's timeless teachings, when rightly understood and applied, bless all of humanity with everlasting wisdom and perpetual joy."

Shloka 6: Divine Navigator: Krishna, a Boatman Across Life's Tumultuous River

भीष्मद्रोणतटा जयद्रथजला गान्धारनीलोत्पला
शल्यग्राहवती कृपेण वहनी कर्णेन वेलाकुला |
अश्वत्थामविकर्णघोरमकरा दुर्योधनावर्तिनी
सोत्तीर्णा खलु पाण्डवै रणनदी कैवर्तकः केशवः || (6)

bhīṣmadrōṇataṭā jayadrathajalā gāndhāranīlōtpalā
śalyagrāhavatī kṛpēṇa vahanī karṇēna vēlākulā |
aśvatthāmavikarṇaghōramakarā duryōdhanāvartinī
sōttīrṇā khalu pāṇḍavai raṇanadī kaivartakaḥ kēśavaḥ || (6)

"Bhisma and Drona form the riverbanks, Jayadratha its flowing waters, Shakuni emerges as the blue lotus, while Shalya lurks as the shark. Kripa represents the river's swift currents, with Karna as its fierce waves. Ashvatthama and Vikarna are its daunting killer whales, and Duryodhana, its treacherous whirlpools. Through this tumultuous river of battle, the Pandavas navigated safely, for Krishna was their guiding boatman." (*Gita Dhyanam: 6)*

The Daunting River of Life's Challenges

Life is often compared to a river—ever-flowing, unpredictable, and full of challenges. The Mahabharata war is a poetic representation of a river filled with complex challenges that even the bravest hearts find hard to face, let alone overcome. Through a subjective analysis, let us see how each character from within the Mahabharata storyline individually symbolizes various challenges.

Bhisma and Drona are likened to the river's formidable banks. Jayadratha to its deceptive flow. Shakuni, the misleading blue lily, the ruthless speed of Kripa's currents, Karna's rough breakers, and the lurking dangers of Ashvatthama, Vikarna, and Duryodhana are always ready to pull one under.

Krishna: The Guiding Boatman in the Storm

What hope do the Pandavas have for this perilous journey? Their only redeemer is Krishna, *Kaivartakaḥ*, the skilled boatman. Good mariners need to be equipped with complete knowledge of the boat and proficient skills to navigate unforeseen waters under them, no matter how turbulent. Krishna is glorified here as a boatman of sound wisdom and unwavering equipoise who can guide us safely through life's most testing times.

Protector of the Helpless: A Reservoir of Hope

The flow of life events has an intensity and force of its own. Trapped in its fierce currents, one often feels cornered and helpless. But even and especially in the darkest moments, when all seems lost, the eternal glimmer of hope shines forth as Krishna. He is devoutly hailed as *ārta trāṇa parāyaṇā* or the protector of the despondent and vanquished. His enlightening teachings assure us that there is always a way through or around even the most insurmountable challenges.

Surrender to the Ultimate Guide

Life's continuous onslaught of challenges overwhelms even the best of us. At such times, the ability to surrender to Krishna's love and wisdom comes from profound understanding. It requires entrusting ourselves to a guide with unparalleled knowledge and incredible foresight. It is developing, through experience, the faith that with Krishna steering our ship, we can better navigate all tempestuous waves. As we continue to exert prudent self-effort and put our trust in this Divine navigator despite overwhelming challenges, he illuminates paths we never knew existed, leading us to newfound hope and serenity.

In 1964, Mary Stevenson, an evangelist who traveled the world with her husband for more than 25 years, was caught at a crossroads in life, lost for direction. One day, she saw a cat's footprints in the snow and scribbled down 20 lines that became the immortal poem *Footprints in the Sand,* which continues to inspire millions worldwide.

Her poeticized story beautifully accentuates the underlying message of this *shloka*. The gist of the poem is:

One night, a man dreamed he was walking along the beach with the Lord. He noticed two sets of footprints. However, during the saddest times of his life, there was only one set of footprints. The man questioned the Lord about this. "I don't understand why, when I needed you the most, you would leave me." The Lord replied, "During your times of suffering, when you saw only one set of footprints, it was then that I carried you."

Summary

This evocative *shloka* offers a metaphorical representation of life's challenges using the imagery of a treacherous river and stresses the essential role of Krishna in our journey. Life, as we have all experienced, is not a placid stream but a tumultuous river with unexpected hurdles at every bend. Yet, in and through this unpredictable voyage, a beacon of hope exists in the form of Krishna. His time-proven teachings are potent tools to help us cross the river of life. Adhering to Krishna's guidance means while keeping our efforts alive, surrendering our fears and doubts to an Intelligence greater than our own. It means allowing Him to reveal the solutions to our dilemmas. We are never utterly lost when we trust him to steer our ship, even in the stormiest waters.

"Life's challenges may be relentless, but with Krishna as our navigator, no wave is indomitable."

Shloka 7: Celestial Lotus: The Mahabharata's Luminance

पाराशर्यवचः सरोजममलं गीतार्थगन्धोत्कटं
नानाख्यानककेसरं हरिकथा सम्बोधनाबोधितम् ।
लोके सज्जनषट्पदैरहरहः पेपीयमानं मुदा
भूयाद्भारतपङ्कजं कलिमलप्रध्वंसिनः श्रेयसे ॥ (7)

pārāśaryavacaḥ sarōjamamalaṁ gītārthagandhōtkaṭaṁ
nānākhyānakakēsaraṁ harikathā sambōdhanābōdhitam |
lōkē sajjanaṣaṭpadairaharahaḥ pēpīyamānaṁ mudā
bhūyādbhāratapaṅkajaṁ kalimalapradhvaṁsinaḥ śrēyasē || *(7)*

"May the immaculate lotus of the Mahabharata, born from the words of Parashara's son Vyasa, with the profound meaning of the Gita as its fragrant essence and its myriad tales as stamens, unfurled by the enlightening stories of Lord Hari, be joyfully savored day after day by the wise of the world, akin to honeybees. This very lotus, which wipes clean the stains of the *Kali-yuga*, may it always be for our highest good. "(*Gita Dhyanam*: 7)

Shloka 7 is a hymn celebrating the magnificence of the Mahabharata. More than just a tale, this lyrical melody describes the epic as a radiant lotus of wisdom blossoming in the vast lake of ancient knowledge.

Mahabharata: The Glimmer of Hope in the Age of Strife

The current age, *Kaliyuga,* often described as the age of discord, finds its redemption in the wisdom of the Mahabharata. In an era dominated by ego and selfish pursuits, *Kaliyuga*'s nature personifies the shadowy recesses of humanity. Amidst this unconquerable chaos, the Mahabharata is a repository of very pragmatic teachings that guide hearts adrift and illuminate the path to nobility and righteousness. This monumental work articulates personal, social, and political ethics, presented through an intertwining collection of very captivating stories. The lessons contained in the Mahabharata, if duly imbibed, facilitate our physical, emotional, intellectual, and spiritual evolution.

A Blooming Lotus: The Pristine Grandeur of the Mahabharata

Visualize the Mahabharata as a brilliant lotus budding from the oceanic depths of Vyasa's words. This is not portrayed as an ordinary lotus—it is *amalam*, untouched by impurities. The flawless nature of its narratives, the perfection of its language, and the sanctity of its teachings make the Mahabharata come forth in a captivating bloom.

The intoxicating fragrance of this divine lotus, likened to the powerful teachings of the Bhagavad Gita, lures noble minds from every corner. Just as a lotus comprises countless petals, the Mahabharata is enriched with myriad sub-stories, each bearing immense significance. Some of these tales, like glinting gems, have been extracted, polished, and displayed separately by scholars in various works.

But what causes the lotus to bloom in its whole grandeur? It is the presence of the sun. Similarly, the presence of Krishna sanctifies and renders the stories of the Mahabharata useful. Without Krishna's luminous touch, the Mahabharata would remain a beautiful but unopened bud.

Nectar for the Intellect: Embracing the Wisdom

The honeybees hover over every flower that holds nectar. Similarly, the Mahabharata, with its profound teachings on *Dharma*, psychology, values, ethics, and human relationships, attracts *sajjanaṣaṭpadaiḥ*, or seekers of truth. These seekers, like honeybees, draw ravenously from the Mahabharata's reservoir of wisdom, returning day after day to quench their insatiable thirst for knowledge.

Every petal of this luminous lotus, called the Mahabharata, is a life-altering lesson. Every whiff of its diffusive fragrance is a guiding principle, and every drop of nectar is a transformative insight. May the fragrant profundity of its timeless wisdom uplift us into more evolved states of awareness.

Summary

Shloka 7 exalts the Mahabharata's brilliance, metaphorically painting it as a pure lotus emerging from the depths of Sage Vyasa's profound wisdom. This epic, with its ethical tales, combats the challenges of *Kaliyuga*'s moral decay. The Bhagavad Gita's teachings hold the fragrance of the lotus, while its myriad stories act as enticing filaments, drawing seekers of truth. Krishna's presence vitalizes this epic, rendering the wisdom relatable and transformative. The Mahabharata stands as an eternal compass, guiding generations through life's complexities.

"As the lotus thrives amidst murky waters, so does the Mahabharata shine, guiding souls through Kaliyuga's shadows."

Shloka 8: Echoes of Divine Grace: Turning Impossibilities into Realities

मूकं करोति वाचालं पङ्ग लङ्घयते गिरिम् |
यत्कृपा तमहं वन्दे परमानन्दमाधवम् || (8)

mūkaṁ karōti vācālaṁ paṅguṁ laṅghayatē girim |
yatkṛpā tamahaṁ vandē paramānandamādhavam || (8)

I bow to Lord Krishna, the Lord of Lakshmi (Wealth), Brimming with supreme joy. By His grace, the mute speaks eloquently, And the lame ascend mountains. (*Gita Dhyana Shloka: 8)*

Shloka 8 has embedded within its heart-stirring poetry a reminder of the boundless grace of the Almighty. It is a clarion call to humanity to face and overcome all challenges. Through all indomitable adversities, it assures us of the compassionate benevolence of Divinity embodied here as *Bhagavan* Shri Krishna.

We can tap into this boundless reservoir of love, hope, and strength through sincere devotion and complete surrender.

Salutations to Madhava: The Multifaceted Luminary

Salutations to the splendid Madhava, the very personification of *Paramananda,* the supreme joy. The name Madhava weaves diverse interpretations that bear profound spiritual significance.

The Sovereignty of Resources

The syllable *Ma* in Madhava represents the power of Goddess Lakshmi, the epitome of wealth and prosperity, and *Dhava* signifies her consort or beloved. While Lakshmi symbolizes the limitless wealth of the universe, her union with Madhava makes him, as it were, the supreme custodian of all resources.

A Symphony of Silence and Meditation

Further exploration of the meaning of this name leads us to its more profound spiritual connotation. Madhava also finds its roots in the Sanskrit terms *Mauna* (silence) and *Dhyana* (meditation). Adhering to this reference, Madhava is the Divine essence realized through silent introspection and meditative contemplation.

The Sweetness of the Divine

The endearing allure of Madhava is often compared to the sweetness of honey. Every characteristic of Krishna is drenched in this sweetness, making him irresistibly charming. The intoxicating lyrics of the *Madhurashtakam,* composed by Srimad Vallabhacharya in praise of this captivating sweetness of Madhava, describe how every facet of the Divine is pure, sweet joy.

Through these varied and compelling interpretations, we are left with no doubt that the core of Madhava is *Paramananda.* His boundless nature requires no external trigger for manifestation. There is an innate state of contentment, eternal joy, and infinite happiness. And He bestows this enduring joy upon those who seek His grace.

Prayer: A Bridge to the Divine

This *shloka* is a beautiful prayer, a bridge connecting us to the boundless grace of Madhava, the Divine. It assures us of the transformative power of genuine surrender and devotion. Prayer is a very potent action. And, like every action, it has results. The outcomes of such heartfelt prayers are either palpable and immediate or unseen and more subtle.

The immediate boon of such prayers is instant psychological pacification. Uttering a prayer is a testament to our capacity to aspire, yearn for, and seek the higher. The act of prayer validates a fact that we are all consciously or unconsciously aware of—that we are not alone nor helpless within the undefinable expanse of the cosmos. While everything we lean on in this mortal world is impermanent, transient, and undependable, in Madhava, we find an everlasting, unflinching, and reliable pillar.

Madhava is abundant in resources, omnipresent in nature, omnipotent in strength, and omniscient in his compassion. The assurance that, within this vast universe, there is an entity that never falters and never disappoints gives us unparalleled solace.

This assurance is the immediate benefit of our prayer, which enlivens us with renewed vigor, a reinforced spirit, and an enlightened perspective. But beyond what can be seen and felt lies the ineffable grace that gently envelops our being, guarding and guiding us every step of the way.

Grace: The Divine Alchemy

If prayer is a bridge to the Divine, grace is the unseen path illuminated by that connection, which leads to manifold subtle or apparent blessings. Emerging organically from the bosom of prayer, grace reveals itself as a tangible reality in our lives.

Grace is the indirect, ethereal boon of our prayers. It is not some whimsical gift sprinkled from the heavens, but a consequence, a reward that is rightfully earned. The universe operates on the immutable principle of cause and effect. What we perceive as grace is essentially *karma-phala,* the fruit of our actions. Every prayer, as every deed, sows a seed, the fruition of which we see as grace. It is bestowed upon us not on random whims but because of our own deeds, our *karma,* whether recent or from a distant past.

Yet, the beauty of grace lies in its unpredictability. There are moments when we cannot directly correlate a blessing to a deed. In such instances, where outcomes surpass our expectations and situations miraculously turn in our favor, we genuinely witness the alchemy of Divine Grace. Grace works its magic in unthinkable ways, such as turning obstacles into stepping stones, making the mute eloquent, and enabling the lame to scale mountain peaks.

Mute speaking and lame climbing mountains may seem like an exaggeration to the intellectual mind. But think! In and through our lives, we all aspire to remarkable goals that we feel are impossible to attain. Given our resources, talent, and capacity, perhaps they are. But this *shloka* assures us that even the impossible is made possible when we put in the right effort and humbly surrender to the grace of the Divine.

Indian Saints and spiritual luminaries have unceasingly extolled the transformative potency of this Divine Grace. Sri Ramakrishna Paramahamsa, one such beacon of wisdom, explains this phenomenon with a poignant analogy. He describes Divine Grace as a perpetual wind, ever-present, constantly blowing. Yet, he says, we must unfurl our sails to harness this boundless energy. The boat of our lives remains stagnant, not for lack of grace but because we've yet to set sail to catch its winds.

"Unfurl your sails," Ramakrishna Paramhansa urges, "then you will catch the wind and move forward. That much work we must do to experience grace." [27]

Besides familiarizing us with the power of Divine Grace, this *shloka* also induces a sense of deep humility within us. It tempers our arrogance toward doership. We each may be excellent at what we do, but it subtly reminds us that we can do what we do only with the power of the Divine. Without the might of this power, we are all rendered incapacitated. So, in a way, it teaches us to acknowledge and bow down to this power before and through any undertakings, never forgetting that the Divine Hand leads our way and the Divine Will fulfills all our *sanklapas* or resolves.

There is a thought-provoking story in the Kenopanishad about how *Agni Devata* (the presiding deity of fire) and *Vayu Devata* (the presiding deity of wind) were incapacitated when Divinity withheld its power due to their arrogance. Despite employing all their might, neither could burn or blow away a tiny leaf.

By reflecting on and reciting this verse, we reach out to the very heart of the cosmos. We longingly cry out to the Divine. We salute *Bhagavan*, the enigmatic force by whose grace the impossible is made possible. It is a heartfelt acknowledgment of the transformative power of grace, a humble plea to experience it, and a reminder that with humility, faith, devotion, and concerted effort on our part, this universal force will always conspire in our favor.

Summary

Shloka 8 is a sincere prayer to the Divine, an invocation to tap into the boundless source of grace. At its helm stands *Ishvara*, with all his expertise, the custodian of all the resources of the universe. His grace possesses the alchemy to render the mute eloquent and empower the lame to scale towering peaks. Through this prayer, we not only benefit from the psychological solace that comes from aligning with a supreme force that is unparalleled in power, but we also receive the unseen boon of grace to attain whatever we set our hearts to. This prayerful *shloka* brings to the fore the miraculous power of Divine Grace when one is surrendered at its altar with humility.

Surrender to the Divine, and grace will make the unthinkable your reality.

Shloka 9: Harmony of the Cosmos: Reverence to the Eternal Ishvara

यं ब्रह्मावरुणेन्द्ररुद्रमरुतः स्तुन्वन्ति दिव्यैः स्तवैः
वेदैः साङ्गपदक्रमोपनिषदैः गायन्ति यं सामगाः ।
ध्यानावस्थित तद्गतेन मनसा पश्यन्ति यं योगिनः
यस्यान्तं न विदुस्सुरासुरगणाः देवाय तस्मै नमः ॥ (9)

yaṁ brahmāvaruṇēndrarudramarutaḥ stunvanti divyaiḥ stavaiḥ
vēdaiḥ sāṅgapadakramōpaniṣadaiḥ gāyanti yaṁ sāmagāḥ |
dhyānāvasthita tadgatēna manasā paśyanti yaṁ yōginaḥ
yasyāntaṁ na vidussurāsuragaṇāḥ dēvāya tasmai namaḥ || (9)

"To the Supreme *Ishvara*, extolled by Brahma, Varuna, Indra, Rudra, and the Marut through celestial hymns; The Very One celebrated by the singers of the Samaveda, who sing in harmony with the traditions of *pada* and krama, and the Upanishads; The One who reveals Himself to contemplatives when their minds, immersed in meditation, become one with Him;

Whose profound nature remains a mystery even to celestials and demons — to such a Lord, I offer my salutations. "(*Gita Dhyana Shloka 9*)

Shloka 9 reverentially acknowledges the formless Supreme *Ishvara*, the foundational pillar of the universe. *Ishvara*, who is an embodiment of existence (*Sat*), consciousness (*Chit*), and contentment (*Ananda*), not only enlivens every being but is the very source of understanding and transcendence. The *shloka* bursts forth into a goosebump-inducing symphony of the admiration and praise that three highly esteemed luminaries of the universe, the *devas*, scholars, and yogis, shower upon *Ishvara*.

Luminescence of the Devas: Aligned with the Cosmic Order

In whatever way it is understood, the polysemous term *Deva* incites the imagery of sheer effulgence in any seeker's mind. Depending on the context, it could mean a deity, natural laws, or even a sense organ, but the Supreme *Ishvara*, worshipped here, is the All-Knowing *Deva*. Way beyond the grasp of human understanding, the nature of this *Ishvara* is an enigma even to the highest celestial beings.

The *shloka* heralds praise for *Ishavara* from *devas* like Varuna, Indra, Rudra, and Marut, each symbolizing various natural phenomena from rain to wind. This posits an intriguing idea: All-natural laws harmonize with the universal order radiated by the Supreme *Ishvara*, like yarns that weave together the cosmic fabric.

Melody of the Learned: The Vedic Odes to Ishvara

The Veda is an unparalleled body of knowledge that meticulously unravels the nature of the Supreme *Ishvara*. Vedic scholars who journey into its unfathomable depths find their guiding light in *Ishvara*.

Whether rendered in the straightforward sequence of pada or the paired continuity of krama, Vedic chanting is not a mechanical ritual but a profoundly reverential offering. Reciters of the Sama Veda, firmly anchored in sacred knowledge, purposefully infuse their chanting with adoration for *Ishvara* in a way that intonationally elevates the vibration of every hymn.

And then, there are the Upanishads, the crowning jewels of the Vedas. These revered scriptures distill and elucidate the essence of the Supreme *Ishvara*, guiding seekers on their path to Self-discovery. The Vedas recognize and celebrate *Ishvara* while empowering scholars and chanters to be the eternal porters of His divine message.

Echoes from the Depths: The Yogi's Inner Vision

The *shloka* introduces us to another group of spiritual seekers, the Yogis, who commune with *Ishvara* through meditative endeavors. These spiritually introverted individuals journey deep within themselves to grasp the essence of *Ishvara*. In the hallowed silence of their contemplation, they distinctly perceive *Ishvara* as the very essence of their consciousness. In the stillness of their meditation, they discern and unite with the One Supreme *Ishvara*.

Summary

Shloka Nine casts a reverential spotlight on the singular Supreme *Ishvara* who commands the adoration of the cosmos. The all-knowing Lord, elusive in His profound nature, is exalted in the celestial harmonies of the *Devas*, who sing His praise and align seamlessly with His cosmic dictates. Through their meticulous chants and profound understanding, the Vedic scholars praise His glory, while Yogis, in their deep meditative trance, palpably experience His divine presence. The verse offers salutations to that unparalleled force that resonates in every corner of the universe, from the grandeur of deities to the heartbeats of contemplatives.

"Ripping through the vastness of galaxies or the immaculate rhythm of a single heartbeat, there lies the anchoring note of one Supreme Musician who binds the universe in perfect harmony."

Connecting Hearts with the Gita and Its Timeless Tradition

The *Gita Dhyanam* is a series of nine deeply meditative verses preceding the Bhagavad Gita. Devotional recitation of these divine *shlokas* before commencing the study of the Gita makes the mind receptive to the immensity of the knowledge to follow.

These inspiring *shlokas* introduce us to the spiritual treasures buried within the Bhagavad Gita and the Mahabharata. They shine the torch upon the path to Self-discovery we are about to embark upon.

The *Gita Dhyanam* is blessed with the potential, as it were, to invoke Divine presence. Like a heartfelt prayer, each *shloka* echoes a seeker's innermost aspirations, arousing a deep-seated spiritual yearning. In response to that cry, the powerful depiction of Krishna emerges from within its magical poetry, with a whip in one hand and the *Jnana Mudra* in the other—an assuring symbol of guidance for man's worldly endeavors and wisdom to facilitate his inner spiritual retreat.

The *Gita Dhyanam* fortifies our bond with the ancient teaching tradition. It reminds us of our extraordinary spiritual lineage, with a special acknowledgment of Vyasa, the sage who blessed humanity with the invaluable wisdom of the Bhagavad Gita. By reviving this connection with our sacred heritage, the Gita Dhyanam infuses our spirit with a keen sense of humility and gratitude, deepening our reverence for the Gita.

To summarize, the *Gita Dhyanam* is not merely a preamble to the Bhagavad Gita. It is a resounding reminder of the transformative power awaiting us. As we revel in the warm embrace of its contemplative solace, may the insights echoing through its melodious lyrics prepare us well to receive the full import of Gita's life-transforming message.

Arjuna Vishada Yoga

The Journey Begins: Understanding Arjuna's Grief

"Within the womb of our deepest struggles lies the impetus to birthing our greatest transformations."

Having earnestly invoked the grace of the Divine through an in-depth understanding of the *Gita Dhyanam*, we are now ready to begin the study of the Bhagavad Gita.

Chapter One, titled *Arjuna Vishada Yoga,* or The Yoga of Arjuna's Dejection, commences our passage into the core teachings of this sacred text.

We will first paint the grand tableau of the Mahabharata backdrop to set the scene for the intimate dialogue between Krishna and Arjuna to unfold. We will then delve into the profound symbolism of the Kurukshetra war and unravel the layers of Arjuna's inner turmoil. Through a vivid verse-by-verse analysis of Chapter I, we aspire to offer a thorough overview of the human predicament symbolized by Arjuna's despondency and introduce our readers to the transformative potential of despair.

Setting the Stage: Backdrop of the Mahabharata

A pertinent central message and the dramatic context in which that message is delivered are two critical aspects that qualify wisdom as timeless.

The core message of the Bhagavad Gita acknowledges and addresses typical human challenges and illuminates a pathway to inner harmony and Self-realization despite them. The Gita's eternal teachings are a compass for the human journey and have proven their potency and applicability across all time and space.

A compelling background or stimulating context helps bring any esoteric wisdom to life so that it resonates deeply with the human psyche. Contexts are dynamic. They evolve with time, circumstances, and culture. They provide a stage upon which eternal wisdom can be dramatized to make it more accessible and relatable. In his infinite wisdom, Sage Vyasa chose the theatrical background of the Mahabharata and cleverly weaved the teachings of the Gita into the tapestry of this epic civil war.

Yet, it is crucial to understand that while the Mahabharata provides a particular context, the Gita's teachings transcend it. The directives disseminated on the ancient battleground of Kurukshetra is equally applicable in a modern-day corporate boardroom or a quiet suburban household. The vividness of the context might shift, but the underlying wisdom remains steadfastly constant.

Journeying forward, we must remain anchored in the central message of the Bhagavad Gita even as we wholeheartedly revel in the magnificence of the Mahabharata's captivating storyline.

The Mahabharata infallibly reflects the entire spectrum of the human experience. Spanning an impressive 85,000 verses, it is not just the world's most extensive epic but a reservoir of ancient wisdom and ethics.

The Mahabharata, the brainchild of the illustrious sage Vyasa, reveals the very core of *Sanatana Dharma* in vibrant detail. Seekers often wonder why Vyasa felt the urge to write the Mahabharata after compiling the Vedas. The Vedas, compiled first, appear sufficient to shepherd individuals along life's diverse paths. Their comprehensive teachings seem adequate to equip humanity with means and methods to balance material aspirations and spiritual pursuits.

But think! When noble ideals find representation through the lives, tribulations, and choices of individuals, they become tangible and resonate deeply with the student. *Dharma* is the central teaching of the Vedas and the Mahabharata. The ancient Sanskrit saying, *Vedokhilo Dharma Moolam*, emphasizes that *Dharma* is the bedrock of the Vedas. Vyasa beautifully animates this ethereal concept with compelling dramatization, right through the Mahabharata.

The epic masterfully narrates countless scenarios in which *Dharma* is embraced, revered, and sometimes fiercely challenged. It poignantly illustrates the consequences of our choices. It glorifies the peace experienced from upholding *Dharma* and blatantly displays the chaos that ensues when it is forsaken.

Let us briefly glean over segments of the Mahabharata directly connected to the Kurukshetra battle. Our aim is not an exhaustive recounting of the Mahabharata but rather a brief overview to explain the immediate backdrop of the Gita.

Upholding *Dharma*: The Gold Standard of King Bharata

The Mahabharata chronicles the illustrious lineage of the Kuru dynasty, which epitomized *Dharma* in the columns of Indian history. Students of the Bhagavad Gita would do well to familiarize themselves with this antiquity.

King Yayati was a significant figure in the Kuru Dynasty. Puru was one of many of his sons. Yayati aged prematurely due to a terrible curse upon him. He asked his sons to gift him their youth. Only Puru agreed to do so. Pleased with Puru's sacrifice, Yayati chose him as his successor and heir. Puru's clan came to be known as the Puru Dynasty.

Many generations after King Puru, an exemplary king named Kuru was born in the Puru dynasty. King Kuru was known for his virtues, righteousness, and commitment to *Dharma*. Through severe ascetic penances, he brought prosperity and fame to his kingdom. So, while the dynasty began with King Puru, King Kuru's exceptional governance and administration made it famous as the Kuru dynasty.

King Bharata was another bright star of the distinctive Kuru Dynasty. He was born of the union between King Dushyanta and Shakuntala. Bharata's reign exemplified *Dharma* and left an indelible mark in the archives of time. So profound was his influence that the land over which he ruled took on his name, and to this day, the nation of India is known as *Bharatam* in his honor.

What set King Bharata apart was not merely his outstanding regime but also his revolutionary views on leadership. In an era dominated by birthright, he envisioned a kingdom where succession was not determined by ancestry but by merit. It was not a hollow doctrine; he practiced what he preached. In an unprecedented move that solemnized his commitment to *Dharma,* Bharata bypassed his own bloodline in favor of a worthy successor. For him, the throne's legacy was enshrined in the principles of sterling leadership, unwavering commitment to *Dharma*, and a genuine dedication to the nation's welfare.

This benchmark set by King Bharata becomes critical as we explore the backdrop of the Mahabharata battle. It underscores the profound ethos that shaped the narrative and the complexities of the epic's central characters. It highlights the lofty ideals that were the foundation of this ancient civilization.

The Strain on *Dharma*: Bhishma's Fateful Vow

The gold standard of leadership set by King Bharata kept ablaze the torch of *Dharma* and illuminated the path of the entire Kuru dynasty.

Among them was King Shantanu, who, in his prime, was blessed with a very virtuous son, Devavrata.

The narrative's intricate design caught Shantanu's heart trapped by the allure of Satyavati, the daughter of a fisherman chieftain. Yet, love's journey was a complex one. Conditions were set that would challenge the very essence of Bharata's legacy. For Satyavati to marry Shantanu, Devavrata and his entire bloodline would have to relinquish all claims to the kingdom, and the throne would be inherited solely by Satyavati's descendants.

Driven by love for his father and a longing to see him content, Devavrata pledged something many would laud as the pinnacle of sacrifice. He vowed never to claim the throne and to remain untouched by marital bonds to ensure that no offspring of his would ever challenge Satyavati's children for kingship. This is how he came to bear the moniker *Bhishma,* which translates as "he of the terrible or dreadful oath."

Yet, this "noble act" deeply fractured the very spirit of *Dharma.* While Bhishma's promise was a testament to his unwavering devotion to his father, it simultaneously flouted the age-old principle championed by Bharata. How could one preordain the worthiness of unborn rulers, bypassing the golden rule of merit over lineage? Helplessly bound by his love and loyalty, Bhishma unintentionally sowed seeds that would grow into towering trees of conflict and discord.

This singular moment, where unbridled emotions clouded the clear waters of *Dharma,* set into motion a series of unprecedented events that would foreshadow the Mahabharata battle. It is a haunting reminder that even the most well-intentioned actions can have dreadful consequences, especially when they drift away from the established ideals of righteousness.

Challenges of Succession: The Kuru Legacy Tested

After King Shantanu's demise, the Kuru dynasty faced a lot of turbulence. Chitrangada and Vichitravirya, Shantanu, and Satyavati's sons were being prepared to inherit the grand legacy before them. But life's unpredictable turns brought tragedy in quick succession. Chitrangada was killed on the battlefield, while Vichitravirya lost his life prematurely to illness, neither having left an heir for the kingdom. Hastinapura's majestic throne remained barren, and Bhishma, restrained by the chains of his vow, could not ascend to it.

In all her wisdom and foresight, Satyavati turned to the ancient customs for a solution. She beckoned her eldest son, Vyasa, born of her union with sage Parashara. Satyavati entrusted him with the responsibility of perpetuating the Kuru dynasty with the widows of Vichitravirya, Ambika, and Ambalika through the *Niyoga* practice. However, this imposed union was not spared its unexpected outcomes. Ambika, intimidated by Vyasa's intense presence, closed her eyes in fright, resulting in the birth of Dhritarashtra, who was born blind. Ambalika, on the other hand, grew pale during her encounter with Vyasa; thus, a very pale-complexioned son, Pandu, was born to her.

The question of a suitable successor to the throne began to plague the kingdom. The duties of a king were vast and often required the acute perception that comes with physical sight. Dhritarashtra's blindness, despite him being the older of the two, was an outright handicap that disqualified him from claiming the throne. Adhering to the tenets of *Dharma*, which always emphasized capability over birthright, the elders saw Pandu as a more befitting candidate. Therefore, the onus of leadership was placed upon Pandu's shoulders, honoring the principles established by King Bharata and prioritizing merit over mere lineage.

Decisions and Their Echoes

Hastinapura flourished under Pandu's glorious rule. His marriage to Kunti and Madri ensured the continuation of the dynasty. Simultaneously, blind Dhritarashtra wed Gandhari, who voluntarily blindfolded herself out of intense empathy for her husband. Their union was marked by Gandhari's brother, Shakuni, who nurtured a deep-seated hatred toward the Kuru dynasty.

A cloud loomed over Pandu's joy. A hasty act in the forest led to the unintentional killing of Sage Kindama, incurring a curse: should Pandu embrace his wife in passion, death would claim him. This dire impediment forced Kunti to use a divine boon gifted to her by sage Durvasa, by which she could invoke any deity to conceive a child immaculately. By invoking the grace of *Yama*, *Vayu*, and *Indra*, *Kunti* gave birth to Yudhishthira, Bhima, and Arjuna, respectively.

Having received Kunti's remaining boon at Pandu's behest, Madri bore twins Nakula and Sahadeva by invoking the grace of the twin deities *Nasatya* and *Darsa*, collectively known as the *Ashvins*. However, the impact of the curse could not be shaken off. A moment of passion with Madri became Pandu's tragic undoing. In her grief, Madri ended her life, leaving Kunti to raise all five Pandavas.

After Pandu's untimely demise, Bhishma, the guardian of Hastinapura's heritage, brought Kunti and her sons back to the palace. The Pandavas grew alongside Dhritarashtra's hundred sons, led by the ambitious Duryodhana. The complexities surrounding lineage, legacy, and *Dharma* sparked the beginnings of a tragic conflict that would rip apart the very heart of the kingdom.

Choices and Consequences

In the palace halls of Hastinapura, the murmurs around power and ascension grew louder. While Dhritarashtra's heart longed to see Duryodhana, his son ascend the throne, the principles of *Dharma* tilted the balance in favor of Yudhishthira. He was anointed the crowned prince for his unwavering commitment to righteousness and the voice of the people behind him.

Vengeance and ambition lingered as shadows over the destiny of Hastinapura. Shakuni, the puppeteer behind Duryodhana's every evil move, engineered a perilous trap for the Pandavas by constructing an inflammable palace. But Vidura's wisdom saved the Pandavas from a grievous end. Believing the Pandavas perished in the treacherous *palace of lac*, Hastinapura's court hastily declared Duryodhana as their crowned prince. The apparent rise from the ashes of the Pandavas following the palace incident and Arjuna's unabashed display of prowess at Draupadi's *swayamvara* gave rise to a political challenge: Hastinapura now had two crowned princes. A decision rooted in pacifism divided the kingdom: Duryodhana held Hastinapura's reins, while the Pandavas created their paradise in Indraprastha. By adhering to *Dharma* and through sheer dedication, the Pandavas transformed a chunk of barren ground into Indraprastha – a land of unparalleled prosperity. While the Pandavas found contentment in their domain, envy continued to gnaw at Duryodhana.

Duryodhana's ambition, backed by Shakuni's cunning, hatched a plot to lure Yudhishthira into a game of dice. Although aware of the moral pitfalls of such a game, Yudhishthira regrettably compromised his *Dharma*. The dice, manipulated by deceit, stripped the Pandavas of their wealth, kingdom, and honor. A period of exile was decreed. As the Pandavas ventured into the wilderness, each moment was a lesson, a preparation. With Krishna's guidance, they sought reconciliation and their rightful place on their return. But Duryodhana's **hardened** heart refused them even a grain of soil, let alone a kingdom, setting the stage for a horrific clash that would echo through the aisles of history. The balance of *Dharma* swayed, awaiting a reckoning.

On the Brink: Readying for Kurukshetra

Once expansive and hopeful, the horizon of peace began to narrow for the Pandavas. Every path of diplomacy had been walked, every plea for justice voiced, but Duryodhana's heart remained steadfastly unmoved. The drums of war began to roll. The Kauravas amassed a compelling army of 11 *Akshauhini* or battalions. Among their ranks were legends like Bhishma, bound by duty to Hastinapura; Drona, the remarkable mentor whose allegiance was to the throne, not necessarily its occupant; and Karna, the unsung hero tethered by his loyalty to

Duryodhana. Some secretly harbored sympathy for the Pandavas, but their obligations and circumstances pulled them into the Kaurava fold.

The Pandavas rallied a humbler force of seven *Akshauhini,* or battalions. But where they lacked numbers, they triumphed in spirit and righteousness. Backing their resilience was Krishna. More than a charioteer or friend, he was the embodiment of *Dharma*, a guiding luminescence capable of steering lives through the stormiest seas of mortal existence.

This elaborate web of alliances, motivations, and profound human emotions set the stage for the monumental battle of Kurukshetra. A confrontation destined to gauge more than mere martial skill—its outcome would reveal the very core of morality, integrity, and *Dharma*.

Zooming in to the Context of the Gita

The Kurukshetra Conundrum

At the break of dawn, an alarming stillness enveloped the vast expanse of the Kurukshetra battlefield. Two colossal armies, representing kinship and enmity, stood facing each other. The choppy swish of fluttering flags, blaring trumpets, and the call of conches ripped through that ominous stillness. The warriors were ready to engage in a battle that would reshape history. The Kaurava army, with 11 *Akshauhinis*, boasted a formidable display of might, while the Pandavas, though lesser in number with seven *Akshauhinis*, exuded an undying spirit of righteousness.

Arjuna, the third Pandava prince and the linchpin of their strategy was seated in his majestic chariot, driven by none other than *Bhagavan* Shri Krishna. With the Gandiva bow firmly held, he was a picture of power, certainty, and victory. The outcome of the war heavily hinged on his performance. Upon his request, Krishna positioned their chariot between the two armies so Arjuna could gauge the strength and morale of his adversaries. However, the faces of grandfathers, teachers, cousins, and cherished friends dotting the enemy lines at once crumbled his resolve to fight. The actuality of a battle against his own and the unbearable weight of potential loss shook him to his core. The bow slipped from his grasp, and a crippling despair consumed him.

The great sage Veda Vyasa chose this profoundly intense moment to bless humanity with the life-transforming message of the Bhagavad Gita. Arjuna, aware of the dharmic reasons for this war and his crucial role in it, was incapacitated beyond retrieval at zero hours of battle. He knew he would face beloved elders like Bhishma and mentors like Drona on the battlefield. Yet, the immediacy of the situation, the reality of taking arms against people he loved and revered, overwhelmed his senses. From standing firm as a symbol of bravery, Arjuna melted into a puddle of doubt and sorrow. This pivotal juncture sets the foundation for the Bhagavad Gita—a dialogue between Krishna and Arjuna that would forever guide individuals through life's most intimidating challenges.

A Battlefield for Life's Lessons

The sprawling plains of Kurukshetra, with its array of armored warriors and the cacophony of war drums, may seem an unusual setting for a riveting spiritual discourse. But this was a deliberate backdrop that the revered sage Vyasa chose for the Bhagavad Gita. In an unfamiliar student, it naturally stirs intrigue as to why.

From time immemorial, profound spiritual insights were often delivered amidst tranquil settings: under ancient trees, beside serene lakes, or nestled within the tranquility of mountains. While no doubt conducive to unhindered receptivity, the repeated choice of these quiet environments has unintentionally conveyed that spirituality thrives only in seclusion, away from the tumultuous rhythms of everyday life. But Vyasa's Gita dispels this notion. His battlefield context animates a potent message that, in truth, spiritual teachings are not only meant to revel in unruffled moments of calm but prove to be practical tools to transcend utter chaos and spiritually evolve from it.

By positioning the Bhagavad Gita amidst the chaos of war, and more so, a civil war fraught with moral dilemmas, Vyasa brilliantly highlights that spirituality is not a retreat from reality but an engagement with it. It is not confined to temples or secluded ashrams but is even more necessary in marketplaces, homes, offices, and, yes, even battlefields. This dramatic background makes the Gita a testament to the enduring relevance of spiritual wisdom. It challenges us to find peace not just in moments of solitude but amidst the very challenges that rattle us, emphasizing that actual spiritual growth is achieved when we carry these teachings from the quiet corners of contemplation into the undulating peaks and valleys of our everyday lives.

Arjuna: Everyman's Prototype

The reality of human existence finds resonance in Arjuna's grief-stricken condition. This celebrated warrior, esteemed for his unmatched prowess, is confronted with a heart-rending circumstance on the battlefield of Kurukshetra: a call to arms against loved ones. Beyond the din of rolling chariot wheels and war drums, Arjuna's internal strife echoes the eternal human conflict between choice and duty.

It is not merely about drawing an arrow or sheathing it; Arjuna's inner turmoil mirrors our vulnerable moments. His confused despair reminds us of the executive torn between pursuing profit and ethical practices, a doctor deciding between two equally crucial surgeries with limited resources, a student choosing between passion and practicality in a career, or a parent balancing between being a friend or a disciplinarian to a child.

Different eras and myriad challenges, yet an irrefutable commonality binds them together: the daunting choice between moral and ethical dilemmas. Throughout history and every occupation of life, a Kurukshetra will exist, with choices demanding clarity and conviction. The enlightening wisdom enshrined within the Bhagavad Gita will continue to help us master our emotions and make intelligent choices anchored in *Dharma*.

The Battle Within- A Mirror to Our Inner Struggles

The Mahabharata war is not just a mere historical event. It is a vivid allegory of the eternal struggle within each of us. Every day, a Kurukshetra battle plays out in the vast expanse of our minds. Here, Arjuna symbolizes you and me wrestling with many, often conflicting desires and yearning for clarity amidst the fog created by our unrelenting wants. His faltering bow, Gandiva, reflects our own moments of doubt and weakness.

In the Kurukshetra battle, the Pandavas emerge as the champions of nobility and virtue. They represent our noble thoughts and uplifting emotions that guide us toward the path of *Dharma*. The Kauravas, overwhelming in number, symbolize the countless harmful thoughts and tumultuous sentiments that attempt to divert us from our true purpose. There is a glimmering ray of hope amid this internal turbulence - Krishna. He is the guiding voice of wisdom and clarity within us, constantly nudging us toward decisions rooted in *Dharma*. The backdrop of Bhagavad Gita is not just recounting an age-old battle. Its thorough understanding will assist us in identifying, confronting, and gaining victory over our inner conflicts to experience a more purposeful existence."

Arjuna Vishada Yoga: Despair as the Prelude to Enlightenment

The Bhagavad Gita begins with a chapter aptly named *Arjuna Vishada Yoga*. To the uninitiated, melding the terms *Vishada* and *Yoga* might appear paradoxical. After all, in conventional wisdom, *Vishada*, or despair, is seldom seen as a precursor to Yoga – the path of discipline, union, and spiritual ascension. Yet, as often experienced but sadly overlooked in our own lives, Arjuna's rock-bottom despondency was the catalyst that propelled him toward the pursuit and mastery of Yoga. It validates the fact that the most luminous paths to truth often emerge from the depths of our darkest moments.

Arjuna Vishada Yoga is nestled within the *Bhishmaparva* of the grand Mahabharata and comprises 47 verses. The teachings within this chapter are divided into two salient segments:

Verses 1-27: Against the backdrop of the Mahabharata, these verses artfully draw parallels to the broader human experience. Here, the depth of the human dilemma is interwoven with historical dramatization, allowing readers to glean their own reflections within the age-old chronicles of warriors and kings.

Verses 28-47: This segment unveils the very core of our shared struggles, shedding light on the manifestations of fundamental human weaknesses. It is an in-depth introspection into Arjuna's psyche and, through him, into the mind of every individual.

The call of the great master Paramahamsa Yogananda echoes poignantly through this chapter: 'Find out what you are - because you want to make yourself what you ought to be.' [28] Before striding toward our grander Self, we must first fully comprehend our present state. The first chapter helps us primarily identify and acknowledge our internal struggles. It emphasizes the universal truth that understanding the problem is the initial, crucial step toward its resolution.

It is essential to realize that Arjuna Vishada Yoga is more than an exposition of a warrior's internal conflict. It is an invitation to all of us to acknowledge and comprehend our own inner battles. Approaching this chapter with this understanding, we open ourselves to an inspiring and transformative journey that the literary and spiritual genius of the Bhagavad Gita promises.

Arjuna Vishada Yoga: Verse-by-Verse Analysis

As we have seen earlier, the first chapter of the Gita is not merely an introduction to the epic Mahabharata battle but delves deep into the intricacies of human emotions and mortal struggles. In our verse-by-verse analysis, we will interpret its teachings both in the context of the Mahabharata and the inner struggles we all face. This dual lens offers a comprehensive understanding of the Gita's timeless wisdom, emphasizing its significance in historical and personal contexts.

Shloka 1: From Blindness to Clarity: The First Stride Toward Insight

धृतराष्ट्र उवाच -
धर्मक्षेत्रे कुरुक्षेत्रे समवेता युयुत्सवः |
मामकाः पाण्डवाश्चैव किमकुर्वत सञ्जय ||1||

dhṛtarāṣṭra uvāca -
dharmakṣētrē kurukṣētrē samavētā yuyutsavaḥ |
māmakāḥ pāṇḍavāścaiva kimakurvata sañjaya ||1||

Translation:

Dhritarashtra asked:

"O Sanjaya, assembled in the dharmic land of Kurukshetra and desiring battle, what did my sons and the sons of Pandu do?" *(Arjuna Vishada Yoga: 1)*

Commentary:

The Bhagavad Gita discourse commences with Dhritarashtra, the blind old king, posing a simple question to his loyal charioteer, Sanjaya. This innocuous query carries greater significance than is gleaned at first sight. The Mahabharata narrative unfolding upon the vast expanse of the Kurukshetra battlefield mirrors the intertwining complexities of our own lives — wherein our myriad thoughts, desires, and inclinations constantly jostle for dominance.

Vyasa's dramatic portrayal of Dhritarashtra creates a compelling backdrop. Refusing the gift of vision offered by the revered sage Vyasa, Dhritarashtra chooses to remain in darkness and rely instead on Sanjaya's divinely bestowed sight to receive an unfiltered account of the unfolding drama. Why did he decline the gift of sight for himself?

Deep down, Dhritarashtra sensed the imminent defeat of his sons, knowing fully well that they were not even remotely aligned with the principles of *Dharma*. Yet, his unconquerable attachment to them clouded his better judgment, disabling him to stand for what is just and right. The term *mamaka*, which translates as 'my people,' plainly proclaims Dhritarashtra's possessive love for his sons. It highlights his unwillingness to detach from his familial bonds and view the scenario with neutrality.

While conversing with Vyasa, Dhritarashtra confessed to knowing the path of *Dharma* or righteousness yet found himself swept away by the prevalent currents of moral compromise. We can all identify with this sentiment. How often are we fully acquainted with the right course of action and yet are swayed by prevailing societal norms or personal attachments?

Sanjaya, in stark contrast, embodies discernment and clarity. Gifted with the capacity to see beyond the ordinary, he stands firmly on the flank of unbiased truth. Many of our journeys through life are tinged with Dhritarashtra's metaphorical blindness — an inability to discern right from wrong due to overpowering attachments and biases. Hence, it becomes imperative to seek our own Sanjaya — a guiding voice, be it an individual or an inner moral compass- that can provide clarity amidst life's chaos.

This opening verse of the Gita shines light on Dhritarashtra's desire for clarity. His inquiry, despite his biological blindness, is evidence of a deep yearning to understand the unfolding events. His selection of Sanjaya as his guide is noteworthy. *Sanjaya* is not just a charioteer; he exemplifies honesty, objectivity, and unwavering loyalty. Dhritarashtra's eagerness to comprehend the occurrences in Kurukshetra proves crucial at this point. Without this keen inquiry and a genuine readiness to know, the wisdom of the Gita would remain undisclosed.

This verse carries a powerful reminder: *the first step toward progress is a sincere desire to understand.*

Inner Mirrors: Kurukshetra's Reflections Within

While deeply interwoven with historical anecdotes, the unfurling tenets of the Bhagavad Gita offer an introspective lens that urges us to minutely examine our inner psyche. The Kurukshetra battlefield's historical setting reflects the contradictions and conflicts that continually churn within us.

"If the broad expanse of Kurukshetra symbolizes the eclectic theater of our life, its warriors personify the thoughts, emotions, and tendencies that challenge each other within our minds. Just as a blind Dhritarashtra represents ignorance, so are we often unaware of our physical, emotional, intellectual, social, and spiritual states. Like Dhritarashtra, we lose sight of *Dharma* or the righteous path, and clouded by biases and attachments; we inadvertently perform adharmic or unrighteous actions.

Consider our daily struggles. How often do we introspect and genuinely scrutinize the influences that govern our decisions? It is easy to float along the river of life, passively succumbing to external pressures and internal whims. But the very first *shloka* asks us, albeit in a barely audible whisper, 'Do you truly know what is transpiring within?'

When we turn our gaze inward, we are exposed to a realm teeming with thoughts of various hues—some constructive, others not. We realize how we are tossed about by all sorts of fleeting emotions, all triggered by diverse events and experiences. We feel joy, pain, love, envy, calmness, and rage. But how often do we pause to recognize the patterns amid this mental discord? To understand which emotions or thoughts provide a forward-moving drift to our ship and which ones try to capsize it?

Here is where symbolism plays such a significant role. The Kauravas, born of Dhritarashtra's blindness, represent those thoughts and emotions that are self-serving and often detrimental, stemming from our mind's inability to discern right from wrong. They are the clamorous temptations, the bursts of irrational anger, and the bouts of baseless pride.

On the opposite side stand the Pandavas, exemplars of discernment and righteousness. If the Kauravas drown us in a mire of confusion and chaos, the Pandavas uplift and guide us toward clarity and purpose. They represent those moments wherein we surrender to humble acceptance of our flaws, adequate self-restraint, and the surge of genuine love.

We are reminded of a proverb whose origins are murky. It has been attributed to Christian pastor Billy Graham in 1978 as well as the Cherokee Native American tribe, as shared below:

Two Wolves: A Cherokee Legend [31]

An old Cherokee is teaching his grandson about life.

"A fight is going on inside me," he said to the boy.

It is a terrible fight, and it is between two wolves. One is evil; he is anger, envy, sorrow, regret, greed, arrogance, self-pity, guilt, resentment, inferiority, lies, false pride, superiority, and ego."

He continued, "The other is good—he is joy, peace, love, hope, serenity, humility, kindness, benevolence, empathy, generosity, truth, compassion, and faith. The same fight is going on inside you—and inside every other person too.

The grandson thought about it for a minute and then asked his grandfather, "Which one will win?"

The old Cherokee simply replied, "The one you feed."

The play of our lives is a Kurukshetra, a battlefield where these opposing forces constantly clash. And depending on which power within us gains prominence at any given moment, our mental state shifts, influencing our reactions, decisions, and actions.

The hope lies in acknowledgment. Just as Dhritarashtra's inquiry marks a yearning for clarity despite his blindness, conscious self-introspection is the first step toward understanding and consequent transformation. When we begin to investigate our mental processes and recognize the dominant forces at play within us, we kickstart the journey from mindless existence to purposeful living.

The transformational message of the Gita guides us to upgrade our *Kurukshetra,* our field of action, to *Dharmakshetra,* where actions align with righteousness. This does not imply a utopian state of perpetual positivity. Instead, it emphasizes the harmony born of awareness, understanding, and mastery over our inner world.

Although the Kaurava forces dominated the Pandava armies in numbers, much like the negative tendencies do the positive ones within us, as history stands witness, battles are not won solely on the merit of strength but by strategy. Understanding the terrain, the warriors, and the stakes is the first step toward devising a winning game plan. In the context of our inner lives, it means crafting an intelligent and productive way of living for ourselves.

Shloka 1 calls for self-introspection and urges us to chart the territories of our minds. To discern which qualities of ours serve us and which do not. The tendencies we empower within unquestionably dictate the life we experience without.

Historical and symbolic Significance:

Within scriptural epics, as seen in the Bhagavad Gita, the names of various characters are not just identifiers; they hold deep historical, linguistic, and symbolic significance. By understanding the meaning of each name, especially in the context of each *shloka,* we will develop a more comprehensive appreciation of the text.

Dhritarashtra: The Blind Monarch of Mind and Matter

Historical Aspect: Dhritarashtra, a prominent character in the Mahabharata, was the father of the Kauravas and the paternal uncle of the Pandavas. As seen earlier, he was born to sage Vyasa and queen Ambalika and has been blind since birth. This physical handicap declared him unfit to rule the kingdom, so his younger brother Pandu ascended the throne. However, after Pandu's premature death, Dhritarashtra became the de facto ruler, albeit always in contention due to his disability and unyielding attachment to his sons.

Linguistic Interpretation: *Dhritarashtra* can be broken down into two Sanskrit words: *Dhrita,* which means 'held' or 'sustained,' and *Rashtra,* meaning 'nation' or 'kingdom.' Thus, *Dhritarashtra* translates to 'he who holds or sustains a kingdom.' It is an apt name for a character who, despite his physical handicap, retained a firm grip on the reigns of his kingdom, both in terms of his actual rule and his emotional attachments.

Symbolic Meaning: Symbolically, Dhritarashtra represents humanity's blindness to spiritual truths. [28] The kingdom he clings to represents the body, or material existence. His attachment to this kingdom of the body points out our own attachments to physical and material pleasures, often at the cost of spiritual growth. His blind mind, which gives birth to the Kauravas (representative of destructive emotions and tendencies), signifies the dangerous consequences of living a life guided by a conscience that lacks spiritual discernment. Just as Dhritarashtra's blindness to his sons' unrighteous inclinations led to the catastrophic Kurukshetra war, our unchecked emotions and attachments, born of spiritual ignorance, can lead to internal turmoil and external discord.

Dhritarashtra's characterization cautions us against allowing the blind mind, bereft of wisdom and discernment, to govern our desires and actions. It implores us to cultivate inner vision, ensuring that our efforts in the world are guided not by transient emotions but by the impeccable principles of *Dharma*.

Sanjaya: The Introspective Seer of Truth

Historical Aspect: Sanjaya's role as the narrator of the divine dialogue between Krishna and Arjuna on the Kurukshetra battlefield earns him a key position in the Mahabharata storyline. He was born to the divine sage Gavalgana and later became King Dhritarashtra's charioteer and adviser. He was a faithful disciple of Sage Vyasa and displayed unwavering devotion to his duties in the service of the Kuru dynasty. Vyasa endowed Sanjaya with the divine gift of distant vision, which allowed him to view and impartially narrate the events unfolding on the battlefield of Kurukshetra.

Linguistic Interpretation: For better understanding, the Sanskrit word *Sanjaya* can be split into *Sam*, meaning 'completely,' and *Jaya*, meaning 'victory.' *Sanjaya* thus translates to 'one who is completely victorious' or 'wholly triumphant.' This name effectively captures the essence of his unbiased character, which conquers ignorance and rises above misjudgments owing to the clarity of his intellect.

Symbolic Meaning: *Sanjaya,* within the context of the Bhagavad Gita, symbolizes thorough self-introspection. [28] While Dhritarashtra represents a mind clouded by ignorance and attachment, *Sanjaya* exemplifies the higher intellect or the discerning aspect of our personality. His divine ability to see events from a distance alludes to the clarity of vision that comes from keen self-introspection. It highlights our ability to detachedly witness our thoughts, emotions, and actions from an elevated perspective. The precision and truthfulness of his narration stress the importance of being true to ourselves, which can only happen when we recognize our strengths and acknowledge our weaknesses in all honesty.

In Shakespeare's Hamlet, "*This is above all; to thine own self be true. And this must follow as the night follows the day. Thou canst not then be false to any man,*" is the famous advice King Claudius' chief minister Polonius gives his son Laertes, who is leaving his father's home for university."

Sanjaya's character encourages us to rise above petty emotions and biases, look at the bigger picture, and always consider the repercussions of our choices. Just as he narrated the events of the war without corrupting them with personal judgments, we, too, are urged to observe our lives more objectively and act with sound discernment.

In summary, *Sanjaya's* name and character teach us that amid life's many battles, only honest introspection, guided by higher wisdom, can steer us onto the right path, following which we can attain complete victory over our internal adversaries.

Kurukshetra: The Battlefield of Life's Choices

Geographical and Historical Aspect: Kurukshetra, a region in modern-day Haryana, India, holds great historical and spiritual significance. It is primarily recognized as the battlefield for the Mahabharata War, upon which culminated a colossal conflict between the Pandavas and the Kauravas. Kurukshetra is also revered as sacred ground and continues to draw countless pilgrims from all over the world. Having silently absorbed the timeless wisdom of the Bhagavad Gita delivered by Krishna to Arjuna more than 5,000 years ago, Kurukshetra is a living testament to India's spiritual legacy.

Linguistic Interpretation: The Sanskrit word Kurukshetra is derived from two words: Kuru, which refers to the Kuru dynasty (that which both the Pandavas and Kauravas hail from), and Kshetra, which means 'field' or 'domain.' Thus, Kurukshetra translates as 'the field of the Kurus.' But contextually, Kshetra also implies the idea of an 'arena of activities' or a 'domain of action.'

Symbolic Meaning: Metaphorically, Kurukshetra reflects the vast expanse of our inner world. It embodies the field of our actions, where our thoughts, emotions, and desires combat each other daily. Just as the Kauravas and Pandavas clashed on this battlefield, our internal contradictions – virtues against vices, aspirations against apprehensions, personal affinities against duties – lock horns, vying for dominance. In this context, our body becomes a stage for all these mental activities. If we are not tethered to truth and harmony within, our body thoughtlessly animates the more powerful of these warring tendencies, leading to internal and external chaos.

Kurukshetra reminds us that life is not about gaining victory over external battles; the source of all conflict lies within. It stresses the role that introspection, spiritual alignment, and self-awareness play in guiding our actions in this ever-dynamic field of life. When we adhere to our *Dharma*, or righteous duty, our internal *Kurukshetra* effortlessly transforms into *Dharmakshetra*. Our body then serves our life purpose as a finely tuned instrument harmoniously aligned with the universal order. The ultimate message and goal of the Bhagavad Gita are to bring our every thought, emotion, word, and action into thorough alignment with truth and righteousness.

"Along life's perilous terrains, pausing to ask a simple question can often pave the way for profound understanding."

Shloka 2: Whispers on the Wind of Kurukshetra

सञ्जय उवाच -
दृष्ट्वा तु पाण्डवानीकं व्यूढं दुर्योधनस्तदा ।
आचार्यमुपसङ्गम्य राजा वचनमब्रवीत् ||2||

sañjaya uvāca -
dṛṣṭvā tu pāṇḍavānīkaṁ vyūḍhaṁ duryōdhanastadā |
ācāryamupasaṅgamya rājā vacanamabravīt ||2||

Translation:

Sanjaya Observed:

"Observing the disciplined formation of the Pandava forces, King Duryodhana approached his mentor Drona and voiced these words." *(Arjuna Vishada Yoga: 2)*

Commentary:

In response to Dhritarashtra's query, Sanjaya's keen observation immediately cut through the optics to provide an intelligent analysis. His unobstructed vision, void of partiality or prejudice, enabled him to begin narrating the happenings on the battlefield objectively.

Echoes of Strategy and Doubt:

The Pandavas displayed ancient and revered military tactics. The Kaurava prince Duryodhana was taken aback upon seeing this meticulous arrangement of their forces. Their formations, known as *Vyuhas,* were not a superficial show of strength but strategic masterclasses designed to trap the opponent. They were a testament to the Pandavas' foresight, discipline, and preparedness.

Duryodhana, not one to be easily unsettled, clearly feels intimidated by what he is face-to-face with. Instead of withdrawing into quiet introspection or rallying his troops, he strides across to seek counsel from Dronacharya, whose presence on the battlefield is especially symbolic.

Drona, the venerable teacher of both Kauravas and Pandavas, carries an aura that can influence the very tide of the battle. For Duryodhana to approach him on the brink of battle speaks volumes about the prince's state of mind. There is an undercurrent of anxiety, a tremor of doubt. The otherwise haughty and formidable Duryodhana now seeking reassurance is an unexpected sight.

Sanjaya's narration here flings open doorways right into the human psyche. It affirms that when faced with overwhelming odds or the sheer brilliance of an adversary, even the mightiest resolves are intimidated enough to waver. The sight of the Pandava army, their ranks, and files so diligently arranged brings to the surface, as it were, Duryodhana's internal turbulence. It is a fascinating start to what promises to be an epic saga of clashing wills and shifting allegiances.

Through this verse, we realize that something more than brute strength or vast resources fuels the confidence of a leader or a faction. Alignment with righteousness, or *Dharma*, plays a key role. Despite possessing immense strength, if one's actions are not aligned with *Dharma*, doubts creep in and reveal the fragility of misplaced conviction at the most inopportune times.

The Inner War: Virtues, Vices, and the Power of Habit

The second *shloka* of the Bhagavad Gita familiarizes us with our own ongoing inner battles. The profound teachings of Paramahamsa Yogananda and insights from his masterwork, God Talks to Arjuna, help us transition from the objective canvas of the Mahabharata to the subjective intricacies of the human psyche.

As perceived by Sanjaya (our introspective faculty), within the vast terrain of the mind, both *dharmic* and *adharmic* forces vie for dominance. Righteous virtues like self-control, stability, love, devotion, and empathy are potent enough to overpower the dark shadows of our psyche and align us with *Dharma*. [28]

Yet, it is quite an enigma that even amidst the radiant glow of such noble qualities, we often find ourselves led astray by the unrighteous forces within us. The *shloka* iterates this fact vividly: upon witnessing the strength of *dharmic* thoughts, the *adharmic* ideas within us, symbolized by Duryodhana, seek refuge and reinforcement from Drona—our ingrained habits. [28]

Our habits, born from repeated behaviors, steadily become the very fabric of our character. Like the skilled archer Drona, our habits wield tremendous influence. Under their shadow, our actions often become involuntary. While virtuous habits can steer us toward a life of righteousness and inner peace, detrimental habits can blindfold our discerning nature, making us unwitting slaves to our lower selves.

This subtle warning in the second verse of the Bhagavad Gita cautions us that while we might be brimming with *dharmic* intentions, we must remain ever vigilant. If the *adharmic* tendencies within us gain the upper hand, they will, with the support of our habits, eclipse our inherent goodness. The *shloka* nudges us to recognize and reflect upon this internal tug-of-war, this dance of duality.

This *shloka* is a reminder that it is not just about recognizing the divine righteous virtues within us but also about being wary of the age-old habits that might hinder our spiritual journey. Ultimately, this inner alignment with *Dharma*, beyond the shackles of our habitual patterns, paves the way for material and spiritual progress.

Historical and Symbolic Significance of Names from the *Shloka*

Duryodhana

Historical Context: Duryodhana, the eldest son of Dhritarashtra, is a central antagonist in the Mahabharata. As prince of the Kuru dynasty, he led the Kauravas against the Pandavas in the great war of Kurukshetra.

Linguistic Meaning: Derived from the Sanskrit root words *du* (difficult) and *yodhana* (to conquer), the name *Duryodhana* translates as "the one who is difficult to conquer."

Symbolic Interpretation: Duryodhana symbolizes the powerful material passions that govern us. As the leader of destructive emotions and negative thoughts, he represents the challenging internal forces we often struggle to overcome.

Drona

Historical Context: Dronacharya, often referred to simply as Drona, was a Master of Advanced Military Arts and the royal guru of the Kaurava and Pandava princes. Under his unparalleled tutelage, many warriors of the Mahabharata attained perfection in warfare.

Linguistic Meaning: Drona stems from the Sanskrit root *dru,* "to melt." Thus, Drona can be translated as "that which remains in a melted state." [28]

Symbolic Interpretation: Symbolically, Drona signifies the innate urges and habits that constitute our psyche. Every thought we nurture and every action we perform leaves a subtle impression, or "melted footprint," in our unconscious mind. Over time, these imprints crystallize, giving birth to the habits that steer our thoughts, feelings, words, and actions even without our conscious will or volition. [28]

"No matter our skill or the depth of our resources, when unaligned with Dharma, true confidence remains elusive."

Shlokas 3, 4, 5 & 6: The Luminous Legions: Dharmic Forces Within

पश्यैतां पाण्डुपुत्राणाम् आचार्य महतीं चमूम् |
व्यूढां द्रुपदपुत्रेण, तव शिष्येण धीमता ||3||

अत्र शूरा महेष्वासाः भीमार्जुनसमा युधि |
युयुधानो विराटश्च द्रुपदश्च महारथः ||4||

धृष्टकेतुश्चेकितानः काशिराजश्च वीर्यवान् |
पुरुजित्कुन्तिभोजश्च शैब्यश्च नरपुङ्गवः ||5||

युधामन्युश्च विक्रान्तः उत्तमौजाश्च वीर्यवान् |
सौभद्रो द्रौपदेयाश्च सर्व एव महारथाः ||6||

paśyaitāṁ pāṇḍuputrāṇām ācārya mahatīṁ camūm |
vyūḍhāṁ drupadaputrēṇa tava śiṣyēṇa dhīmatā ||3||

atra śūrā mahēṣvāsāḥ bhīmārjunasamā yudhi |
yuyudhānō virāṭaśca drupadaśca mahārathaḥ ||4||

dhṛṣṭakētuścēkitānaḥ kāśirājaśca vīryavān |
purujitkuntibhōjaśca śaibyaśca narapuṅgavaḥ ||5||

yudhāmanyuśca vikrāntaḥ uttamaujāśca vīryavān |
saubhadrō draupadēyāśca sarva ēva mahārathāḥ ||6||

Translation:

"O Revered Teacher! Cast your gaze upon the vast assembly of the Pandava forces, masterfully marshaled by your illustrious disciple, Dhrishtadyumna. Among their ranks, you'll find warriors whose valor rivals that of Bhima and Arjuna. Yuyudhana, the formidable Virata, the seasoned Drupada, the valiant Drishtaketu, and the brilliant Chekitana. The courageous king of Kashi marches with them, accompanied by the fearless Purujit and Kuntibhoja. Shaibhya, the lion among men, is present, as are the courageous Yudhamanyu and Utthamaujas. Not to be overlooked are the brave offspring of Subhadra and Draupadi, all of whom are revered as mighty charioteers." (*Arjuna Vishada Yoga*: 1.3, 1.4, 1.5 & 1.6)

Commentary:

In these *shlokas*, Duryodhana lists one after another the formidable leaders who are the backbone of the Pandava forces. His introduction of the enemy line to Dronacharya, who did not need any as he had trained them all himself, is clearly not a tactical briefing but an overt expression of concern and perhaps a begrudging admission of his awe of them. Each exemplary character called out by Duryodhana has historically displayed unparalleled prowess and valor in warfare.

Dhrishtadyumna: The commander-in-chief of the Pandava army and the one destined to slay Dronacharya. Born out of the sacrificial fire, he was a warrior par excellence, handpicked by Draupadi herself to lead the forces.

Yuyudhana (Satyaki): A stalwart disciple of Arjuna and a Yadava chief, Satyaki's invincible courage paralleled Arjuna's. He could fight any number of warriors single-handedly. His loyalty to Krishna and the Pandavas was unquestionable.

Virata: The noble king of the *Matsyas* The Pandavas and their wife, Draupadi, successfully lived incognito for one year in his palace to fulfill the final condition of their exile. A mighty chariot-warrior, his skills were well-known to all prominent rulers of the era.

Drupada: The king of Panchala and the father of Draupadi. Once a dear friend of Dronacharya, their relationship soured, leading to a bitter personal enmity on the battlefield.

Drishtaketu: Fearless warrior and son of Shishupala, the king of Chedi.

Chekitana: A Yadava hero of the Vrishni clan. He commanded one of the Pandava army's seven *akshauhinis* (battalions).

King of Kashi: Known for the bravery and strength he brought to the alliance, the mighty king of Kashi was a force to be reckoned with.

Purujit, Kuntibhoja: Brothers of Kunti, who was the mother of the Pandavas. These valiant warriors introduced unique strategies to the Pandava camp, strengthening their lineup.

Shaibya: King of the *Shibi* and father of Yudhistara's wife Devika. A lion among men, he was revered for his courage and adherence to the code of a Kshatriya.

Yudhamanyu and Utthamaujas: Brothers and princes of the Panchala territories. These young, mighty, and valiant warriors were known to be as skilled in battle as their gallant predecessors.

Sons of Subhadra and Draupadi:

Abhimanyu: Arjuna and Subhadra's son was a prodigious talent and the apple of everyone's eye. His extraordinary skill of breaking into the *chakravyuha* earned him a revered remembrance in the Mahabharata war.

Draupadi had one son from each of the five Pandava brothers. Though they were young, they were trained by the best and showed signs of becoming great warriors.

1. **Prativindhya:** Son of Yudhistara
2. **Shrutasoma:** Son of Bhima
3. **Shrutakarma:** Son of Arjuna
4. **Shatanika:** Son of Nakula
5. **Shrutasena:** Son of Sahadeva

Maharatha translates as "a great chariot-warrior." A *maharatha* could take on multiple warriors simultaneously, displaying unparalleled martial might. Duryodhana's emphasis on this title sheds light on the grave nature of the challenge he is now forced to acknowledge.

Duryodhana's mention of *Maheṣvāsa* glorifies the significance of legendary bows in the epic. The bows, more than being mere weapons, were extensions of the warriors themselves. Arjuna's *Gāṇḍīva,* for instance, was a symbol of his supreme archery skills and unyielding spirit.

Duryodhana was not merely one by one calling out the Pandava lineup. He was voicing aloud his own overwhelming concern about the array of heroes and legends who stood ready in arms before him to defend the cause of *Dharma.*

Eternal Echoes: From Pandava Valor to Modern Mastery

Through these verses, Duryodhana's deliberate listing of the mighty Pandava forces reminds us of the reservoir of latent powers and *dharmic* tendencies we house within ourselves. If acknowledged and strengthened, these virtuous qualities are equipped and ever-ready to combat the shadows of *adharma* that periodically destabilize our mental and moral equilibrium.

These *shlokas* help us take stock of our internal arsenal. The *dharmic* virtues, subtly represented by the stalwarts of the Pandava army, serve as a moral compass that guides us through life's periodic onslaughts.

Abiding by these *dharmic* values, we are well-equipped to face life's most formidable challenges. Instead of succumbing as victims, we emerge as masters of the situation. Such mastery, fortified by inner strength, can be seen in historical and contemporary figures alike. Their life stories animate for us the power of *Dharma in* action.

Chesley Sullenberger: In 2009, when faced with the harrowing reality of both engines failing mid-air, Captain 'Sully' had a mere 208 seconds (about three and a half minutes) to make a life-or-death-defining decision. The virtues of calmness, focus, and determination he nurtured triumphed as he masterfully landed the US Airways flight on the Hudson River, ensuring the safety of all on board. The serene waters of the Hudson that day mirrored the *dharmic* forces of fearlessness and equipoise that guided Sullenberger through what seemed like an insurmountable crisis.

Mahatma Gandhi: Against what looked to be a never-ending reign of the British Empire on Indian soil, a single man's spiritual wisdom, honesty, fortitude, and commitment set into motion a non-violent revolution. Gandhi's adherence to truth and non-violence was not just a strategic choice but the manifestation of deeply ingrained *dharmic* values. His unwavering faith in these principles empowered an entire nation to rally behind him, eventually bringing down the brutally oppressive colonial rule.

Mahendra Singh Dhoni: Though a world apart, the cricket field witnessed its own Kurukshetra battle in the 2011 World Cup final. With India's top-order batting lineup collapsing, the weight of a billion hopes solely rested on Dhoni's shoulders. His calm demeanor, confidence, and steely determination steered India to victory. Dhoni's calm and collected stance amidst the crushing pressure of the game is a testament to the power of the *dharmic* value of equanimity.

We are reminded of a profoundly stirring poem, *Invictus,* written by William Ernest Henley in 1875 [32]. **Nelson Mandela,** the anti-apartheid leader who was jailed for 27 years for his activism and became President of South Africa in 1994, regularly recited this poem through his arduous prison sentence. The poem lauds the power of inner mastery over outer circumstances that can only come from an unwavering adherence to the *dharmic* qualities within us.

Invictus

Out of the night that covers me,
Black as the Pit from pole to pole,
I thank whatever gods may be
For my unconquerable soul.

In the fell clutch of circumstance
I have not winced nor cried aloud.
Under the bludgeonings of chance
My head is bloody but unbowed.

Beyond this place of wrath and tears
Looms but the Horror of the shade,
And yet, the menace of the years
Finds, and shall find, me unafraid.

It matters not how strait the gate,
How charged with punishments the scroll,
I am the master of my fate:
I am the captain of my soul.

– William Ernest Henley

These *shlokas* no doubt appear like a recount of an ancient story, but they perfectly resonate with our contemporary lives. They teach us that, when recognized and nurtured, the *dharmic* forces within us become lighthouses that will triumphantly steer us through life's stormiest seas.

Historical and Symbolic Significance of the Pandavas

The renowned spiritual teacher Paramhansa Yogananda explains that the Pandavas are not merely historical characters but symbolic representations of profound spiritual principles. [28] These principles guide individuals on the journey of mastery over their matter equipment toward consequent Self-Realization. Each of the Pandavas exemplifies these principles in diverse ways.

Yudhisthira: Divine calmness

Historical Perspective: As the eldest of the five sons of Kunti, Yudhisthira played a crucial role in the Mahabharata, holding the Pandavas together through various trials and tribulations and leading them to eventual victory. He was celebrated for his unwavering commitment to truth and righteousness.

Symbolic Significance: Yudhisthira represents divine calmness. His name, derived from *Yudhi* (war/battle) and *Sthira* (steady/firm), exemplifies someone who remains stable and calm under any circumstance. As *Dharma Putra*, the offspring of *Dharma-Yama* (righteousness), he symbolizes the highest discriminative faculties that compel individuals to stand in truth under all circumstances.

Bhima: Life Force

Historical Perspective: Bhima, known for his unparalleled strength, was a central figure in many of the Mahabharata's epic battles. He possessed immense physical power, being born of the deity of the wind, *Vayu*.

Symbolic Significance: Bhima embodies the power of controlled vitality and life force (*prana*). When directed inward, this energy is potent enough to still the bodily organs, protect one against destructive emotions, and safeguard one from diseases.

Arjuna: Self-control

Historical Perspective: Arjuna, the unrivaled archer, was pivotal in the victory of the Pandavas in the Kurukshetra war. His inner conflict and subsequent enlightenment through *Bhagavan* Shri Krishna's discourse form the essence of the Bhagavad Gita.

Symbolic Significance: Arjuna symbolizes teetering self-control. His incapacitating despondency mirrors the inner conflicts we all confront when pitted against the sensory world. Arjuna is a prototype for every human being trapped in the Kurukshetra battle of life, seeking to gain control over the mind and senses and aiming for spiritual victory.

Nakula: Power of Adherence

Historical Perspective: Nakula, one of the twins born to Queen Madri, was known for his adherence to righteousness, exceptional swordsmanship, and horse-keeping skills.

Symbolic Significance:

Nakula symbolizes the human capacity to live according to virtuous guidelines. This quality, known as *sama*, represents the positive inner power by which uncontrolled mental tendencies can be controlled, helping one walk undeterred on the path of righteousness.

Sahadeva: Power of Restraint

Historical Perspective: Sahadeva, Nakula's twin, was renowned for his wisdom. He was well-versed in astrology and was often consulted for his prophetic insights.

Symbolic Significance: Sahadeva symbolizes the power of restraint. He represents *dama*, the active power of resistance, which helps us govern our restless outer senses. This tenacity to hold back allows us to avoid external distractions and evils and remain focused on our spiritual goals.

In summary, the Pandavas are not just heroes of the Mahabharata epic but embodiments of profound spiritual principles that guide us in our journey toward self-mastery. The historical and symbolic interplay of their characterization helps direct all human endeavors toward *Dharma*.

"Recognition and nurturance of our dharmic essence armor us with the strength and perseverance to be triumphant over life's toughest battles."

Shlokas 7,8 & 9: Echoes of Valor: The Kaurava Vanguard

अस्माकं तु विशिष्टा ये तान्निबोध द्विजोत्तम |
नायका मम सैन्यस्य सञ्ज्ञार्थं तान् ब्रवीमि ते ||7||

भवान् भीष्मश्च कर्णश्च कृपश्च समितिञ्जयः |
अश्वत्थामा विकर्णश्च सौमदत्तिस्तथैव च ||8||

अन्ये च बहवः शूराः मदर्थे त्यक्तजीविताः |
नानाशस्त्रप्रहरणाः सर्वे युद्धविशारदाः ||9||

asmākaṁ tu viśiṣṭā yē tānnibōdha dvijōttama |
nāyakā mama sainyasya sañjñārthaṁ tān bravīmi tē ||7||

bhavān bhīṣmaśca karṇaśca kṛpaśca samitiñjayaḥ |
aśvatthāmā vikarṇaśca saumadattistathaiva ca ||8||

anyē ca bahavaḥ śūrāḥ madarthē tyaktajīvitāḥ |
nānāśastrapraharaṇāḥ sarvē yuddhaviśāradāḥ ||9||

Translation

"Oh, esteemed among the learned, apprehend the exceptional leaders on our side. Here are some prominent commanders in our ranks: yourself, Bhishma, Karna, the ever-victorious Kripa, Ashwatthama, Vikarna, and the son of Somadatta, Bhurisravas. Many other valiant warriors stand ready alongside these heroes, willing to sacrifice their lives for my cause. They are adept with diverse weaponry and are masters in the art of combat." (*Arjuna Vishada Yoga*: 7, 8 & 9)

Commentary

After dramatically introducing the Pandava forces, Duryodhana draws Drona's attention to his own for a comparative analysis, as it were, of the powers at play. This sweeping surveillance of armies uncannily resembles strategic analyses of modern-day sports, business, or warfare, where one evaluates strengths and weaknesses to ascertain a competitive advantage.

Duryodhana's enumeration of the strongest warriors of the Kaurava army boasts the colossal body of might and skill he commands. Some of the foremost warriors he reminds Drona of are:

Drona: A master of Vedas and Vedangas and a great ascetic. He was an unrivaled archer who could fight any number of warriors single-handedly. He taught the art of warfare to the Kaurava and Pandava princes. Duryodhana takes Drona's honorable name first in a flattering effort to subtly remind him of his allegiance and duty to the Hastinapura throne and elevate the spirits of the Kaurava army.

Bhishma: A great personality of infinite knowledge and heroism of the highest order. He possessed mastery over the scriptures and the science of warfare. His incredible personal sacrifice for his father's happiness earned him the boon that even death would not overcome him without his consent.

Kripa: Son of Maharishi Sharadvan, whose allegiance to the throne of Hastinapura was unquestionable. He instructed the Kauravas and Pandavas in archery before the advent of Drona. Many years after the Mahabharata war, he imparted the knowledge of arms to King Parikshit, the son of Abhimanyu and grandson of Arjuna.

Karna: The son of Kunti and God in the form of Sun, Surya. Karna was proficient in the science of arms. He mastered the scriptures and was revered for his exceptional charitable disposition. Duryodhana crowned him King of Angas. Utterly devoted to Duryodhana, he fought on the side of the Kauravas despite his better judgment.

Ashwathama: Son of Drona. He was trained in arms by his father. He was an expert in military science and commanded a portion of the Kaurava army as a *Maharatha*.

Vikarna: One of the hundred sons of Dhritarashtra and also a *Maharatha* in the Kaurava army. He was a virtuous person and celebrated as a great war hero. Vikarna alone opposed Draupadi's persecution in the Kaurava palace, calling it a great injustice.

Bhurisravas: Grandson of Bahlika, who was the elder brother of King Shantanu. He also led the Kaurava army as a *Maharatha.* A righteous person who performed many sacrifices, he was known for his charitable disposition.

Duryodhana does not stop at merely naming each of these mighty Kaurava warriors. He boasts that numerous warriors "are willing to lay down their lives for him." This haughty declaration by Duryodhana echoes the selfish sentiments of his father, Dhritarashtra. There was no concern for the protection of *Dharma* in the father or son. It is worth noting how personal desires and ambition overlook the underlying purpose of a grand war and sideline the greater good.

Duryodhana refers to Drona as the "best among *Dvija.*" In conventional readings, '*Dvija*' is often translated as '*Brahmana.*' However, in this book, we have consciously chosen to avoid terms like '*Brahmana*' and '*Shudra*' as these terminologies, in the modern context, are bitterly associated with a misunderstood caste system. A well-intended societal classification based purely on mental temperaments, due to deliberate and repeated abuse, today has become a social evil that contradicts the teachings of the Gita. At no juncture does the Bhagavad Gita promote caste-based discrimination. Think! If so, Vyasa, the author, and Krishna, the teacher of the Gita, do not come under the *Brahmana* category when viewed through today's caste lens. As seen earlier, Vyasa was the son of a fisherwoman. And Krishna was born to Yadavas. Therefore, to avert any risk of misinterpretation that might distort the vision of the Gita, we define *Dvija* as a 'spiritually oriented person.' This expression better describes an individual's inner disposition, virtues, and actions, negating birth-determined labels.

Many times, we have heard *Dvija* being translated as "twice-born" by various Vedanta teachers. This definition rests on the premise that a person is first born physically from the mother's womb and is born again spiritually when they are formally initiated into or seriously committed to a spiritual path. The second birth is considered more consequential than the first along one's mortal sojourn. This definition sits better with the modern intellect and especially with sincere seekers as it opens this title of *Dvija* to every sincere seeker on the spiritual path.

As we have seen earlier in the Gita Dhyanam, the wisdom of the Bhagavad Gita functions as this spiritual mother that births a spiritually evolved being out of an ordinary one.

Whispers of Inner Shadows: Navigating *Adharma*'s Labyrinth

Duryodhana's description of the valiant Pandava forces transitioning to that of the Kauravas is emblematic of the dual nature of the human psyche. The Kaurava warriors named by him symbolize the numerous *adharmic* tendencies within each of us. And, just as the Kauravas outnumbered and appeared mightier than the Pandavas on the Kurukshetra battlefield, unrighteous tendencies often outnumber and overpower the righteous ones within us.

Adharmic propensities like lust, rage, delusion, blind attachment, aversion, a lack of restraint in speech, greed, pride, envy, arrogance, and hypocrisy vie for dominance within us. Fueled by material passions, they continuously disrupt our inner peace, give rise to unwarranted thoughts and emotions, and pull us off the path of righteousness.

Despite knowing the potential consequences of our actions, we often succumb to these negative inclinations. This human failing is not just limited to our personal lives but is evident across various epochs and cultures:

Despite his unparalleled skills, the valiant Arjuna succumbs to his inner turmoil on the very battlefield he is supposed to conquer.

In Christian theology, despite God's clear mandate, Adam and Eve could not resist the temptation presented by the serpent and lost their place in paradise.

From Greek mythology, despite his father Daedalus' instructions, Icarus flew too close to the sun, fatally falling prey to his hubris.

These stories validate a universal truth: irrespective of our innate wisdom or worldly achievements, our negative inclinations get the better of us.

These *shlokas* are not mere enumerations of various war heroes but reflections of the eternal battle between the higher and lower tendencies warring within us. Recognizing these opposing forces helps us take the first step toward their mastery. In our personal Kurukshetra, the wisdom of the Bhagavad Gita helps us identify and prioritize *Dharma* amidst the pervasive noise of *adharma*.

"It is not the number of notes present in the symphony of the heart that matters but the harmonious melody they bring forth together."

Shlokas 10 & 11: Guarding Bhishma: The Kaurava Crescendo

अपर्याप्तं तदस्माकं बलं भीष्माभिरक्षितम् |
पर्याप्तं त्विदमेतेषां बलं भीमाभिरक्षितम् ||10||

अयनेषु च सर्वेषु यथाभागमवस्थिताः |
भीष्ममेवाभिरक्षन्तु भवन्तः सर्व एव हि ||11||

aparyāptaṁ tadasmākaṁ balaṁ bhīṣmābhirakṣitam |
paryāptaṁ tvidamētēṣāṁ balaṁ bhīmābhirakṣitam ||*10*||

ayanēṣu ca sarvēṣu yathābhāgamavasthitāḥ |
bhīṣmamēvābhirakṣantu bhavantaḥ sarva ēva hi ||*11*||

Translation

"Although our forces, guarded by Bhishma, are vast, they might seem insufficient; while their forces, protected by Bhima, though limited, appear adequately formidable (1.10). Let all of you, strategically positioned in your respective divisions, ensure the protection of Bhishma from all sides (*Arjuna Vishada Yoga*:11)."

Commentary:

The Kaurava Chessboard of War

In *shlokas* 10 and 11, Duryodhana's military assessment familiarizes us with the perception, psychology, and strategy of the Kaurava forces on the battlefield. On the one hand, we have the indomitable Bhishma leading the Kaurava army, which appears unparalleled in numerical strength. On the other, there is the relatively undersized Pandava contingent, stoutly defended by Bhima. This visual comparison of power, however, goes beyond just numbers.

Duryodhana's acknowledgment of his massive forces being possibly "insufficient" despite being led by Bhishma, contrasted against the Pandavas' "adequate" army under Bhima's protection, paints a vivid picture of the nervous apprehensions tormenting the heart of the Kaurava Prince. Here, we sense the subtle undertones of Duryodhana's anxieties. Despite having an army that logically should assure victory, there is an implicit admission of a potential shortcoming.

The essence of this sentiment is captured by the Sanskrit phrase: *arakṣitam daiva rakṣitaṃ; surakṣitam daiva hatam vinaśyati.* This scriptural declaration alludes to the fact that, in the overall workings of the cosmos, divine favor could shield even the unprotected, while its absence might bring down the seemingly invulnerable. In this light, the mere brute strength of the Kaurava army may not be enough.

Duryodhana's call to protect Bhishma under all circumstances is symbolic. Bhishma is not only revered as one of the greatest warriors of the time, but he is a custodian of the Kaurava lineage and its legacy. By urging his commanders to defend Bhishma from all strategic points or ayanams, Duryodhana stresses the need to protect the Kaurava dynasty's honor and prestige.

The word *ayanam*, beyond mere strategic positions, suggests a warrior's station, duty, and commitment on the battlefield. Duryodhana's instruction to his warriors to maintain their *ayanams* affirms his focus on discipline, order, and other quintessential battle details.

Duryodhana's words expose the inner turmoil created by his attention frantically shuttling between military strategy, personal anxieties, and the power of lineage. They give us a peek into the mind of a leader attempting to marshal his forces while grappling with the known and unknown dimensions of the war before him.

The Adharmic Alchemy: Shielding the Pseudo-Self

In all their numbers, the Kauravas symbolize the various impulses, desires, and attachments that often dominate our inner world. These adharmic forces, vast yet not truly sufficient, are led by Bhishma, who here signifies the 'perceived self' or ego. [28] The ego can wield substantial influence fueled by the power of its myriad illusions, misconceptions, and attachments. Just as Duryodhana seeks to protect Bhishma, our internal negative tendencies aim to guard the ego because it is this ego that guarantees their sustenance.

On the other hand, the Pandavas, though fewer but potent, represent the dharmic forces like virtues, proper understanding, and loftier aspirations that guide us toward freedom and enlightenment. Led by Bhima, who exemplifies life force control, they reflect the true strength that emerges from wholly aligning with our higher purpose. While they may seem outnumbered, their inherent power, clarity, and thorough alignment with *Dharma* make them unconquerable.

As explained by Paramahamsa Yogananda in *God Talks with Arjuna*, Bhishma represents more than just a grand figure in an epic tale. His attachment to the Hastinapura kingdom and consequent helplessness under adharmic forces remind us that how we view and understand ourselves plays a pivotal role in shaping our thoughts, feelings, and actions. The journey to Self-Realization becomes arduous if this self-perception is governed by misguided notions.

The strategy of adharmic forces is to protect, nourish, and elevate the ego, putting it in command of our inner world. When the ego reigns supreme, it clouds judgment, fuels desire, and distances us from our true Self.

These *shlokas* subtly yet powerfully highlight the hard-to-comprehend complexities of our internal battle. They teach us that while the external world will unfold as it will, our true purpose and victory lie in mastering our inner world and ensuring that under every circumstance, *Dharma* triumphs over *adharma*, by which we ultimately understand the true nature of the Self. Finally, it is not about the immensity of the forces we have at our disposal but about aligning with the right ones.

"Guarding the ego is the play of our overwhelming negative tendencies which may give us transient outer success, but true enlightenment can be attained by understanding and mastering our inner domain."

Shlokas 12 & 13: Echoes of Kurukshetra: From Battlefield Roars to Inner Wars

तस्य सञ्जनयन् हर्षं कुरुवृद्धः पितामहः |
सिंहनादं विनद्योच्चैः शङ्खं दध्मौ प्रतापवान् ||12||

ततः शङ्खाश्च भेर्यश्च पणवानकगोमुखाः |
सहसैवाभ्यहन्यन्त स शब्दस्तुमुलोऽभवत् ||13||

tasya sañjanayan harṣaṁ kuruvṛddhaḥ pitāmahaḥ |
siṁhanādaṁ vinadyōccaiḥ śaṅkhaṁ dadhmau pratāpavān ||12||

tataḥ śaṅkhāśca bhēryaśca paṇavānakagōmukhāḥ |
sahasaivābhyahanyanta sa śabdastumulō 'bhavat ||13||

Translation:

"Then grandsire Bhishma, the most powerful of the Kuru dynasty, loudly blew his conch shell like a lion to inspire Duryodhana. Then suddenly, a great chorus from conch shells, kettledrums, cymbals, tabors, and cow horn-trumpets sounded; the noise was terrific." *(Arjuna Vishada Yoga: 12 & 13)*

The Lion's Roar and the Ensuing Storm:

The cries of the Mahabharata war echo not just in the tempo of these verses but shriek from the very core of its characters. As Sanjaya transports King Dhritarashtra to the epicenter of the Kurukshetra battlefield, we, too, are given a chance to recognize the convergence of the emotions, strategies, and combat cues arresting our minds.

The ancient battlefield was an outright display of physical prowess and an assertion of emotional and mental fortitude. Bhishma, the grand elder of the Kaurava clan, blows his conch to signal his troops' readiness for war. Sanjaya describes the sound of Bhishma's conch as a lion's roar. A lion, in its majestic might, does not just roar to send a wave of terror through the jungle but also to mark its territory and boost the morale of its pride. Bhishma's conch did precisely that.

Bhishma's blowing of the conch elicited an immediate response from the Kaurava battalions. Just as a single spark can set a forest ablaze, the sound of Bhishma's conch endeavored to reignite the dwindling enthusiasm of the entire army, Duryodhana included. But the reciprocal sounding of the Kaurava conches, drums, and trumpets was neither coordinated nor harmonious; it was tumultuous. It reflected not the strength of unity but warring individualistic ambitions. It revealed, as it were, the fragmentation within the contingent and hung a cloud of gloom and doom over the "mighty" Kaurava side.

The forceful explosion of sounds described here draws our attention to today's unbridled worldly ambitions, which are undoubtedly incredibly impressive but not genuinely constructive for the individual or the collective. There is noise, but is there a melody? There is vigor, but is there direction? As Nataraja Guru aptly puts it, what we hear is an "excited, confused sound," a reflection of the collective conscience of a society veering toward chaos. [30]

The conches and drums are not merely props in historical anecdotes. Alluding to a strict adherence to protocol, even in adversity, the sounding of the conch heralds the commencement of any virtuous endeavor that a code of ethics will govern. Every righteous war has unwritten rules like the battle must be fair, fought face-to-face, and during daylight hours. The foundation of the war carries equal weight as its culmination.

The word *Kuruvriddh* refers to an individual's age, wisdom, and stature. Bhishma's depiction as *Kuruvriddha* highlights his role as the custodian of the Kaurava knowledge, honor, and legacy. *Pratapavan*, translating as splendor and might, describes Bhishma as an epitome of courage and righteousness.

These verses urge us to introspect, align body, mind, and intellect with our highest conscience, and march forward with a clear purpose. The battlefield of Kurukshetra, while ancient, remains ever relevant in its teachings about the human psyche, life strategy, and spirituality.

The Inner Battlefield: Ego's First Trumpet of Turmoil

Let us delve deeper into the more profound significance of these verses. Symbolically, the battle goes beyond the physical terrain and reveals the reality of the human mind that is teeming with dharmic virtues and adharmic tendencies.

Bhishma, the grandsire of the Kuru dynasty, represents our pseudo-self, our ego. Just as Bhishma sounded his conch to invigorate the Kaurava army and got an immediate response, our ego, with its mighty roar, also rallies the adharmic forces within us. The blaring of Bhishma's conch provokes, as it were, those involuntary thoughts that arise unasked, often at the most inopportune moments, unfurling a cascade of further thoughts and emotions.

When we face challenging situations, the pseudo-self, our internal Bhishma, instantaneously stands guard, validating our emotions and making way for a flurry of mechanical thoughts to flood our minds that, unfortunately, become powerful convictions that ambush our mental peace. They create unwarranted anxiety that sees danger at every turn, uncontrolled anger that senses injustice even in benign scenarios, or deep-seated despair that blankets our spirit in hopelessness.

As Paramahamsa Yogananda insightfully conveys, "Material desire wishes past habits, which has sided with the prevailing evil sense inclinations, to be in possession of the full facts about the strength of the opposing metaphysical army." These involuntary thoughts likened to the blaring conches and tumultuous sounds of the Kaurava army are manifestations of our material desires and past habits. They rally with an intensity that often seems insurmountable. They convince us of impending doom brought about by exaggerated imaginary threats, misleading us into impulsive reactions and irrevocable actions.

The clamor that followed Bhishma's conch on the battlefield mirrors the inner chaos that ensues when one unguarded thought triggers a chain reaction. Mindless thoughts come rapidly, one after another, each reinforcing the previous one and creating a turbulent mental environment. Just as the Kaurava army's response to Bhishma's call lacked rhythm and order, our mechanical thoughts too are often irrational, haphazard, and driven by the ego's need to protect and assert itself.

To harness the mind, it becomes paramount to recognize these automatic thoughts for what they indeed are — products of the ego, fleeting and often deceptive. Just as the Pandavas faced the daunting Kaurava army with spiritual fortitude and resilience, we must confront these mental intruders with awareness, discernment, and unyielding faith in our innate *dharmic* strength.

By understanding the nature of this inner Kurukshetra and the soldiers it fields, we can navigate life's challenges not as victims but as conscious warriors, wielding the weapons of self-introspection, awareness, and spiritual wisdom.

"Be it in the stories of ancient clashes or the reality of inner turmoil; true valor emerges not from wielding weapons, but from mastering one's own mind."

Shloka 14: The Luminary's Lore: When Kurukshetra Hears Krishna and Arjuna

ततः श्वेतैर्हयैर्युक्ते महति स्यन्दने स्थितौ |
माधवः पाण्डवश्चैव दिव्यौ शङ्खौ प्रदध्मतुः ||14||

tataḥ śvētairhayairyuktē mahati syandanē sthitau |
mādhavaḥ pāṇḍavaścaiva divyau śaṅkhau pradadhmatuḥ ||14||

Translation

"Then, seated on their magnificent chariot drawn by white horses, Madhava (Krishna) and Arjuna (the Pandava) blew their divine conches." (*Arjuna Vishada Yoga:*14)

Commentary:

Epic Echoes: The Celestial Entrance of Krishna and Arjuna:

In *shloka* 14 of the first chapter, Veda Vyasa, the masterful lyricist, draws readers into a thought-provoking realm where stakes are higher than any earthly conflict through vivid word imagery. The earth trembles beneath the thunderous war signals from the Kaurava forces. Just then, Veda Vyasa swiftly shifts our attention from the howling Kaurava army to the serene yet imposing Pandava side and introduces us to two iconic figures of the Mahabharata epic - Krishna and Arjuna.

Modern directors such as Rajamouli or Quentin Tarantino are celebrated for the dramatic introductions of their heroes, which are known to leave an indelible impression on the audience long after the release of their movies. Similarly, Vyasa's introduction of his two central characters is just as dramatic and unforgettable for students of the Gita. If Tarantino, in 'Django Unchained,' introduces Django as a silhouette against the vast expanse of the Wild West, cluing us in on the character's journey through the film, Vyasa, in his inimitable style, portrays Krishna and Arjuna not just as warriors but as entities who would forever stir within spiritual seekers great spiritual intrigue.

The chariot is described as a *mahati syandane sthitau,* a celestial chariot, pre-empting through a transferred epithet, as it were, the divine roles that both Krishna and Arjuna were to play in this epic war. It also acquaints the readers with the cosmic favors Arjuna had earned through his sincere penance before the war. The chariot, depicting exceptional beauty and strength, was a gift to Arjuna by *Agni Deva* (deity of Fire). Five celestial horses drew this magnificent chariot from among the hundred that were gifted by King Chitraratha. The chariot was said to have the power to travel anywhere on earth or in heaven.

In this verse, Krishna is called Madhava, which acknowledges Krishna's all-encompassing wisdom. As seen earlier, *Ma* means "Mother Lakshmi', the goddess of wealth, and *Dhava* translates as lord. Madhava thus suggests Krishna's lordship over wealth. In this context, wealth implies profound spiritual knowledge, which Madhava Krishna is on the brink of sharing with Arjuna.

Arjuna, a prototype for humanity's eternal confusions and struggles, is aptly named Pandava. Together, they sound their *divyau śaṅkhau* or Divine conches. Apart from being a response to Bhishma's call to war, the sounding of the Pandava conches proclaimed the advent of a dialogue that would eternally help resolve existential human dilemmas.

The *shloka* goes well beyond the description of Krishna and Arjuna, their chariot, or conches. It introduces humanity to the eternal duo, man and *Ishvara*, as *Nara-Narayana*. This relationship, which characterizes supreme wisdom and love, is not only crucial for gaining victory over the inevitable physical battles in life but also assures us of the resolution of the eternal conflict within every human being who yearns for answers and enlightenment.

This *shloka* carries us onto a bygone stage that exhibits both tumultuous battles and profound wisdom—no different than the modern age we experience today.

Discovering the Inner Arjuna: Illumined by the Wisdom of Krishna

This *shloka* introduces us to the probability of a positively conducive alliance within us that patiently awaits our attention despite the ceaseless wars that ravage our minds. Upon the battleground of Kurukshetra, we witness the union of Krishna and Arjuna for reestablishing righteousness. Similarly, through concerted effort, we attain within ourselves a perfect alignment of self-mastery with spiritual wisdom that ensures our evolution.

The chaotic discord within our minds, fraught with desires and distractions, mirrors the force and enthusiasm of the Kaurava army that threatens to overcome us in its wake. But despite this turmoil, every individual possesses an Arjuna, symbolizing one's core strength. This strength, which emerges from self-control, is our intrinsic ability to rein in our emotions and channel them toward greater ideals.

However, self-control bereft of proper understanding stands on unsteady ground and proves useless, if not detrimental, along the human journey. Krishna, the embodiment of spiritual wisdom and the voice of reason is needed to direct our self-control. Spiritual knowledge helps us discern right from wrong, transient from eternal. It ensures that self-control does not cause suppressions and repressions within our bosom but fuels a channeled effort toward progress and Self-Realization.

Through life's arduous journey, it is crucial to identify our inner Arjuna and Krishna. When these two unite, just like they did in the grand epic, the tides of internal battles start turning in our favor, promising a life steered with purpose and graced by peace.

Steering the Inner Chariot: The Ratha Kalpana Illuminated

The vivid imagery presented in *Shloka* 14 carries us into the depths of Upanishadic wisdom. The sight of Krishna and Arjuna on a chariot drawn by white horses is not just a majestic portrait to behold in awe and wonder; it reflects some of the most profound teachings of Indian spirituality.

The significance of the chariot is beautifully described in the *Kathopanishad*, wherein the human experience is likened to a journey on a chariot.

Atmanam rathinam vidhi, Shareeram rathameva tu;
Budhim tu sarathim vidhi, Manah pragrahamevacha.
(Katha Upanishad Chapter 1.3 Shloka 3)

The body is compared to a chariot, and the individual self as its rider. Just as Arjuna's chariot is drawn by the five horses, as described in *Shloka* 14 of the first chapter of the Bhagavad Gita, the five senses pull this human chariot. The ever-fluctuating mind symbolizes the reins that tether the horses. The intellect, endowed with spiritual wisdom, is the charioteer that holds the reins and steers the chariot in the right direction.

Imagine a moment when you are enticed by the aroma of freshly baked pastries. Your senses (the horses) pull you toward the bakery. Resisting may be impossible if your mind (the reins) is let loose. But with a sharp intellect (the charioteer) guided by spiritual wisdom in place, you foresee the implications of your choice. You weigh long-term health benefits against the pleasures of momentary indulgence. You effortlessly resist the tempting pastry and choose a juicy red apple from the neighboring fruit stall to pacify that afternoon sugar craving instead.

When a clear intellect guides the senses and mind, we are assured a smooth journey in life that will forever keep us on track to our intended destination. However, if we allow our senses to roam unchecked, swayed by every whim and distraction, our chariot will run amuck. Wild, untamed horses lead a chariot off track; similarly, unrestrained desires and emotions divert us from our true path.

The symbolism of Krishna, Arjuna, and their wondrous chariot in *Shloka* 14 teaches us to recognize, strengthen, and unite the powers of self-control (Arjuna) and spiritual wisdom (Krishna) within us. When we align our minds and senses with these powers, we clear our path to Spiritual enlightenment.

"Arjuna and Krishna manifest as self-control and Spiritual wisdom within us, and when united, guide us seamlessly through life's challenges."

Shlokas 15, 16, 17, 18 & 19: Pandava's Sonic Sea: Whispers of Virtue

पाञ्चजन्यं हृषीकेशः देवदत्तं धनञ्जयः |
पौण्ड्रं दध्मौ महाशङ्खं भीमकर्मा वृकोदरः ||15||

अनन्तविजयं राजा कुन्तीपुत्रो युधिष्ठिरः |
नकुलः सहदेवश्च सुघोषमणिपुष्पकौ ||16||

काश्यश्च परमेष्वासः शिखण्डी च महारथः |
धृष्टद्युम्नो विराटश्च सात्यकिश्चापराजितः ||17||

द्रुपदो द्रौपदेयाश्च सर्वशः पृथिवीपते |
सौभद्रश्च महाबाहुः शङ्खान्दध्मुः पृथक् पृथक् ||18||

स घोषो धार्तराष्ट्राणां हृदयानि व्यदारयत् |
नभश्च पृथिवीं चैव तुमुलो व्यनुनादयन् ||19||

pāñcajanyaṁ hṛṣīkēśaḥ dēvadattaṁ dhanañjayaḥ |
pauṇḍraṁ dadhmau mahāśaṅkhaṁ bhīmakarmā vṛkōdaraḥ ||15||

anantavijayaṁ rājā kuntīputrō yudhiṣṭhiraḥ |
nakulaḥ sahadēvaśca sughōṣamaṇipuṣpakau ||16||

kāśyaśca paramēṣvāsaḥ śikhaṇḍī ca mahārathaḥ |
dhṛṣṭadyumnō virāṭaśca sātyakiścāparājitaḥ ||17||

drupadō draupadēyāśca sarvaśaḥ pṛthivīpatē |
saubhadraśca mahābāhuḥ śaṅkhāndadhmuḥ pṛthak pṛthak ||18||

sa ghōṣō dhārtarāṣṭrāṇāṁ hṛdayāni vyadārayat |
nabhaśca pṛthivīṁ caiva tumulō vyanunādayan ||19||

Translation

"Krishna, known as Hrishikesha, sounded his conch named *Panchajanya*. Arjuna, known as Dhananjaya, blew his conch, *Devadatta*. The mighty Bhima, famed for his formidable deeds, sounded his majestic conch, *Paundra*. King Yudhisthira, the illustrious son of Kunti, filled the air with the call of his conch, *Anantavijaya*. Nakula and Sahadeva, each in turn, blew their conches named *Sughosha* and *Manipushpaka*. The valiant king of Kashi, the grand archer Shikhandi, Dhrishtadyumna, Virata, and the ever-victorious Satyaki asserted their presence with their conches. Drupada, the offspring of Draupadi and the strong-armed son of Subhadra, also sounded their individual conches. This terrifying sound reverberating through the heavens and the earth tore through the hearts of Dhritarashtra's clan, signaling the commencement of a brand-new epoch." *(Arjuna Vishada Yoga: 15-19)*

Commentary:

Conch Calls of Valor: Resounding Echoes of *Dharma*

These *shlokas* hold our attention upon Kurukshetra, the ground zero of a climactic moral and existential battle. The intermingling sound of war drums and conch shells heralds a monumental war. The response from the Pandava army is distinct and organized, displaying a harmonious union against the clamor of discord from the Kaurava side. The blowing of the conch shells embodies the essence, ethos, and heraldry of the ancient warrior code. Every conch shell has a name that carries the story of the warrior who sounded it.

Sonic Blossoms: The Resounding Echoes of Courage and Bravery

These *shlokas* help us subjectively understand how the contrasting echoes of the Pandava conches represent positive affirmations resounding within the chasms of our minds. The reverberating sound of the Pandava conches is a symbolic heralding of the innate power of positive thoughts pulsating within us. In this allegorical theater, Arjuna's self-mastery and Krishna's spiritual wisdom orchestrate the rhythm of positive vibrations to create a sanctuary of optimism amidst the ruins of despair. The tempo of their conches produces a melody of transcendence attuned to the rhythms of the cosmos. As Paramhansa Yogananda elucidates in his seminal work, God Talks With Arjuna, each conch, with its unique name and resonance, draws us into a spiritual realm of possibilities: [28]

Krishna was the first to respond by blowing his celestial conch, Panchajanya. The sounding of the Panchajanya is a call to *Dharma*, meant to rekindle righteousness within humanity. Its origin traces back to a deed of valor and duty performed by Krishna. It is a reminder of the eternal fight between good and evil and a reassurance of the victory of the good.

Arjuna's Devadatta followed suit and bellowed through the battlefield. Devadatta was a divine gift and symbolizes the grace of self-control and embracing one's higher potential through divine communion. *Devadatta's* cry mirrors the unyielding spirit and resolve of Arjuna, the protagonist whose inner turmoil and moral dilemma are central to the discourse of the Bhagavad Gita.

Bhima's conch, Paundra, is symbolic of the vanquishing of lower tendencies to clear the path for a higher calling. It was a perfect match for Bhima's colossal strength and indomitable spirit. The Paundra reverberated with the ferocity and the boundless courage that Bhima embodied.

Yudhisthira had conquered many kingdoms at the time of the Rajasuya sacrifice. His conch had sounded one victory after another. Thus, his conch came to be called Anantavijayam, which means 'endless victory.' Anantavijayam was believed to conquer infinity and symbolizes the quality of maintaining equanimity and a calm demeanor amidst the storms of life.

Nakula's Sughosha - which means 'sweet-toned' transcends the doubting mind. It propels the mind toward clarity and certainty.

Sahadeva's Manipushpaka - which means 'jewel-blossom,' and signifies manifestation through sound, echoes the idea of focusing one's energies on the fulfillment of all aspirations.

The sounds emanating from the conches of the King of Kashi (modern-day Varanasi), Shikhandi, Dhrishtadyumna, Virata, and the unconquered Satyaki are a representation of the collective consciousness of a righteous resistance against tyranny and moral decay. All these great warriors blew their conches to proclaim their unity and solidarity. The sound produced by the Pandava conches reverberated through the heavens and earth and distinctly differed from the dissonance emanating from the Kaurava conches. This disparity highlights, as it were, the glaring contradiction between transient material desires and the eternal virtues of truth and righteousness. The echo of morality that emanated from the Pandava conches struck terror in the hearts of the Kauravas. The Kaurava conches had no such disheartening effect on the Pandava forces. This striking contrast between the effects of the Pandava and Kaurava conches on each other's morale draws our attention to the superficiality and ephemeral nature of chasing materialistic desires against the depth and congruence of a spiritually integrated life. The divine echo of the Pandava conches that tore through the heavens and earth emphasizes the profound importance of a virtuous life that aligns perfectly with the cosmic vision. Unfortunately, the Kauravas, confined by their myopic vision that rested exclusively on mortal desires, failed to comprehend this truth. The sheer brilliance of this narrative especially calls upon the seeker to diligently introspect and align with the righteousness that is ever-present within. It urges us to rise above the transient and to identify with the eternal.

Hrishikesha: The Cosmic Conductor of *Dharma*

The narrative of Bhagavad Gita, couched within the larger epic of Mahabharata, revolves as much around a life-defining dialogue as it does the deliberate, evocative epithets chosen by Vyasa. The subtle terminology scattered across the verses points to the essence of the characters embroiled in this divine discourse.

Hrishikesha, one of the many wondrous names of Lord Krishna, unfurls its layered significance in a gentle yet thought-provoking manner. Each meaning sheds light on a different facet of the indescribable.

Hrishikesha is primarily heard as the 47th among the thousand venerable names of Lord Vishnu in the Vishnu Sahasranama. Herein, it is traditionally interpreted as the 'Lord of the Senses' or the one under whose command the senses adhere to the call of *Dharma*.

In a subtler vein, Hrishikesha also alludes to the 'rays of joy,' alluding to the luminous entities - the Sun and the Moon. Through this eloquent epithet, by portraying Krishna as the celestial custodian of the Sun that awakens the world to righteous actions and the Moon that cradles it to rest, Vyasa lays the responsibility for the cycle of cosmic activities upon His divine shoulders. The perpetual rhythm of existence, from dawn to dusk, from action to repose, finds its divine conductor in *Hrishikesha*.

The intellectual elegance of *Sanatana Dharma* reveals itself in the beautifully crafted *Vishnu Sahasranama* - a medley of a thousand names, each pointing toward the boundless nature of *Ishvara*. The ancient seers, aware of the infinitude of the divine, embraced the challenge of expressing the inexpressible. They put together numerous pointers, each as a name in the *Sahasranama*, to indicate a unique aspect of *Ishvara*. All thousand names together can be likened to myriad rays, individually and collectively leading to the same luminous core. The

Sahasranama steadily leads us from the known to the unknown, from the finite to the infinite.

In the context of the battlefield, Hrishikesha is not a casual choice of name for Krishna but a deliberate annotation of Lord Krishna's mastery over the senses and the external dynamics of existence. It is a gentle nudge for us to recognize the inherent divine orchestration at play. With *Bhagavan* as the navigator, the Pandavas' chariot is not merely a vehicle of war but a vessel of *Dharma*, cruising through the tumultuous tides of existential dilemmas toward the serene shores of righteous victory. A fratricidal war is thus elevated to a *Dharma Yuddha*, a righteous war, with Hrishikesha, the divine conductor, steering the narrative toward cosmic harmony.

Decoding the Symbolic Nomenclature

The name Dhananjaya for Arjuna is more than a glorification of his material acquisitions. Arjuna is no doubt a victor over wealth, a Master of Resources. Yet, despite the treasures that Dhananjaya amassed, he is helplessly caught in an existential quandary at zero hours of battle. Without the divine guidance of Hrishikesha (Krishna), all his wealth has no meaning and cannot rescue him from incapacitating core human dilemmas. This highlights an enduring teaching of the Bhagavad Gita that, while significant, material triumphs find their true meaning and fulfillment only when aligned with a higher, spiritual understanding.

Bhima's epithets, Bhimakarma and Vrikodara, are meticulously chosen to describe the formidable nature of his being and deeds. *Bhimakarma* - the doer of terrible deeds, reflects his competence and courage in the face of adversity. Whereas *Vrikodara* - the wolf-bellied - symbolizes an unyielding hunger, not just physically but metaphorically, a thirst for justice and righteousness. The imagery of the wolf, always hungry yet ever lean, underscores Bhima's relentless pursuit, even when faced with enormous challenges. His conch, Paundra, befits his larger-than-life presence on the battlefield, sounding out his indomitable spirit.

Yudhishthira, the epitome of righteousness, is aptly referred to as *Raja* - the king. The title not only affirms his rightful position in the kingdom but is a cosmic endorsement of his innate nobility and proper place in the order of *Dharma*. By addressing him as *Raja*, Sanjaya gently nudges Dhritarashtra's conscience, contrasting the legitimate kingship of Yudhishthira with the transient and precarious throne to which Dhritarashtra clings. The appellations *Mahipate* and *Prithvipate* for Dhritarashtra are tacit reminders of the temporary nature of earthly dominion, urging the blind king toward a moral reckoning. As we have seen earlier, the reference to the Bharata lineage highlights an age-old tradition of kingship based on virtue and merit, imploring Dhritarashtra to transcend narrow familial bonds for the larger good.

Vyasa's subtle and layered narrative explores the complex interplay between the earthly and the Divine, the temporal and the eternal. The meticulously chosen names for each character are keys to understanding the multitudinous facets of *dharma* as it unfolds on the grand stage of Kurukshetra. Through this poetic and deeply symbolic nomenclature, the ancient Sage invites us to contemplate the nature of righteous duty as we strive toward a harmonious existence.

These *shlokas* ingeniously remind us of the treasure trove of positive vibrations pulsating within each one of us. With self-control (symbolized by Arjuna) brought under the guidance of spiritual wisdom (epitomized by Krishna), we are able to unleash their power. These positive vibrations, when harnessed and channeled, become our eternal companions through wakefulness and slumber, shielding us from phantoms of negativity.

In conclusion, the objective and subjective revelations within these *shlokas*, sewn together with threads of profound symbolism, elucidate a grand cosmic narrative. The tangible field of Kurukshetra brings to the forefront the subtle intangible battlefields within, where the conches of positivity and spiritual wisdom forever resound, summoning dormant valor to emerge victorious in the relentless pursuit of *Dharma*. Amidst the ruins of despair, the timeless echoes of the conches herald the possibility of a life in alignment with the eternal cosmic order.

"Recognize and empower the positive thoughts within likened to the calls from the mighty conches of Krishna and Arjuna. They will inspire you to face life's challenges with an unwavering spirit."

Shlokas 20, 21, 22 & 23: Warriors' Gaze: Traversing the Battlefield and the mind-Field in the Heart of Kurukshetra

अथ व्यवस्थितान्दृष्ट्वा धार्तराष्ट्रान् कपिध्वजः |
प्रवृत्ते शस्त्रसम्पाते धनुरुद्यम्य पाण्डवः ||20||

हृषीकेशं तदा वाक्यम् इदमाह महीपते |
अर्जुन उवाच -
सेनयोरुभयोर्मध्ये रथं स्थापय मेऽच्युत ||21||

यावदेतान्निरीक्षेऽहं योद्धकामानवस्थितान् |
कैर्मया सह योद्धव्यं अस्मिन् रणसमुद्यमे ||22||

योत्स्यमानानवेक्षेऽहं य एतेऽत्र समागताः |
धार्तराष्ट्रस्य दुर्बुद्धेः युद्धे प्रियचिकीर्षवः ||23||

atha vyavasthitāndṛṣṭvā dhārtarāṣṭrān kapidhvajaḥ |
pravṛttē śastrasampātē dhanurudyamya pāṇḍavaḥ ||20||

hṛṣīkēśaṁ tadā vākyam idamāha mahīpatē |
arjuna uvāca -
sēnayōrubhayōrmadhyē rathaṁ sthāpaya mē'cyuta ||21||

yāvadētānnirīkṣē'haṁ yōddhukāmānavasthitān |
kairmayā saha yōddhavyaṁ asmin raṇasamudyamē ||22||

yōtsyamānānavēkṣē'haṁ ya ētē'tra samāgatāḥ |
dhārtarāṣṭrasya durbuddhēḥ yuddhē priyacikīrṣavaḥ ||23||

Translation:

"Then, O King, observing the formation of the army of the sons of Dhritarashtra, now arrayed and ready for battle, Arjuna, the son of Pandu, whose chariot bore the emblem of the mighty Hanuman, took up his bow, Gandiva, and spoke the following words to Lord Krishna. Arjuna said: O Achyuta (Krishna), kindly position my chariot between the two armies so that I may behold those who stand here eager for battle, with whom I must engage in this great combat. I desire to observe those assembled here to fight, wishing to please the evil-minded Duryodhana in this grand display of war." *(Arjuna Vishada Yoga:*20-23*)*

Commentary:

Arjuna's Moment of Pause: The Precursor to the Gita

From this *shloka* onwards, the narrative shifts from the preparatory buzz of the battlefield to the inner turmoil of our hero, Arjuna. Amidst the war trumpets, the pause, a moment of reflection taken by Arjuna, may seem like an inconsequential happening, but as we will see, it turns out to hold tremendous significance.

Arjuna is referred to as *Kapidwaja* for bearing the emblem of the mighty Hanuman on his chariot, which now stands at the brink of a monumental battle. The reality of the confrontation sinks in when Arjuna is faced with a moral and existential dilemma that is the very foundation of the entire scripture. The readiness for the *shastrasampaate,* or the onslaught of arrows, signifies not just a physical battle but an ethical and spiritual dilemma that is about to unfold.

At this crucial juncture, the external portrayal of Arjuna drawing his revered bow, *Gandiva*, reflects the sound integrity of his conscience as he requests *Krishna* to position the chariot 'between the two armies.' This wish suggests Arjuna's intent to perceive the reality of the war beyond mere formations of ally and adversary. The visual perspective he seeks is not just from a particular placement on the grounds of Kurukshetra but from the standpoint of moral discernment.

The phrase *'yuddhukamaanavasthitan'*, denoting those eager for battle, vivifies the pervasive sentiment on the battlefield. Yet, amidst the frenzy of the ensuing combat, Arjuna's request highlights a discerning mindset, keen on understanding the combatants involved in the conflict rather than being swept by the waves of aggression. This lull before the storm, as it were, where Arjuna wishes to survey the forces on both sides of the battlefield, lays the foundational stone upon which the Bhagavad Gita stands.

Achyuta: The Unswayed Amidst Mortal Turmoil

Arjuna addresses Krishna as Achyuta. This epithet, which translates as 'The Unfallen' or 'The Infallible,' conveys the unblemished, eternal essence of reality that remains untouched by the veils of ignorance or transient worldly illusions. Achyuta is praised in the *Vishnu Sahasranama* (a litany of a thousand names of Lord Vishnu) as the 100th and 318th name, glorifying everlasting purity and undiminished divinity. Arjuna, in addressing Krishna as Achyuta, admits his recognition of the divine wisdom and the unerring guidance that Krishna embodies. At this crucial juncture, where Arjuna finds himself entangled in the quagmire of doubt and moral difficulty, he invokes Krishna as Achyuta exemplifies his quest for an undistorted, transcendent perspective that can illuminate the path of righteousness amidst the shadows of impending conflict. This invocation is a call for clarity amidst confusion and a sincere request to be steered by the 'infallible' through the tumultuous sea of dilemmas. It sets the stage for a profound prelude to a spiritual discourse that will shed light on the realms of duty, righteousness, and the essence of life and death.

Balanced Vision: Unbiased Survey of the Internal Warfront

The sacred dialogue between Arjuna and Krishna in the Bhagavad Gita is an effective channel for exploring the hidden realities of the human psyche. In these *shlokas*, Arjuna is first portrayed as a picture of self-control who stands equipped at the brink of action to begin with and then suddenly hesitates. His hesitation becomes the stimulus for self-mastery and divine counsel to collide.

Upon beholding the forces before him, Arjuna's plea to Krishna as Achyuta cries out a seeker's sincere yearning for boundless wisdom to illuminate the shadows of ignorance that envelope the self. Arjuna's request to position the chariot between the two armies animates humanity's eternal quest to discern the polarities of *dharmic* (righteous) and *adharmic* (unrighteous) tendencies that clash on the battleground of one's inner reality.

Through his request, Arjuna stresses the fact that to traverse the path of spiritual awakening, the seeker must first recognize and confront the assortment of internal forces at play. Be they destructive emotions, thoughts spun from looms of ignorance, impulses driven by blind desires, or other overhanging shadows that reinforce unrighteous tendencies, The battle against these internal foes can only begin when they are clearly seen, acknowledged, and understood.

Arjuna's resolve to confront and understand his internal enemies before engaging in the outer battle demonstrates excellent spiritual insight on his part. Transcendental wisdom, embodied by Krishna, directs self-control, represented by Arjuna. Together, they navigate the turbulent waters of inner conflicts. Backed by the discerning understanding of Krishna, the focused resolve of Arjuna has the chance to translate into right actions aligned with higher truths, freed from the entanglements of ignorance and delusion.

Arjuna's distinct and different moods, as captured in these *shlokas*, artfully reel in a dual narrative. Visually, they portray a skilled warrior's deliberation before a monumental war, evaluating the terrain of conflict and the characters he must engage with. On a subtler level, they reflect every seeker's internal voyage toward Self-Realization. They underline the necessity for self-control to be supported by divine wisdom to successfully navigate the complex, often tumultuous, terrains of inner and outer realities.

"To unlock the potential of ultimate success, we must fortify ourselves with spiritual wisdom and observe our inner battles without prejudice."

Shlokas 24, 25, 26 & 27: Between Heartbeats and Battle Drums: Arjuna's View of the Battlefield

सञ्जय उवाच -
एवमुक्तो हृषीकेशः गुडाकेशेन भारत |
सेनयोरुभयोर्मध्ये स्थापयित्वा रथोत्तमम् ||24||

भीष्मद्रोणप्रमुखतः सर्वेषां च महीक्षिताम् |
उवाच पार्थ पश्यैतान् समवेतान्कुरूनिति ||25||

तत्रापश्यत्स्थितान् पार्थः पितॄनथ पितामहान् |
आचार्यान्मातुलान्भ्रातॄन् पुत्रान्पौत्रान्सखींस्तथा ||26||

श्वशुरान्सुहृदश्चैव सेनयोरुभयोरपि |
तान्समीक्ष्य स कौन्तेयः सर्वान्बन्धूनवस्थितान् ||27||

sañjaya uvāca -
ēvamuktō hṛṣīkēśaḥ guḍākēśēna bhārata |
sēnayōrubhayōrmadhyē sthāpayitvā rathōttamam ||24||

bhīṣmadrōṇapramukhataḥ sarvēṣāṁ ca mahīkṣitām |
uvāca pārtha paśyaitān samavētānkurūniti ||25||

tatrāpaśyatsthitān pārthaḥ pitṝnatha pitāmahān |
ācāryānmātulānbhrātṝn putrānpautrānsakhīṁstathā ||26||

śvaśurānsuhṛdaścaiva sēnayōrubhayōrapi |
tānsamīkṣya sa kauntēyaḥ sarvānbandhūnavasthitān ||27||

Translation:

O King Dhritarashtra, upon Arjuna's request, Krishna stationed the splendid chariot amidst the two armies. They stood before Bhishma, Drona, and all the notable rulers of the earth. Krishna then spoke, "Behold, Arjuna, assembled here are all the members of the Kuru dynasty." Arjuna saw before him, standing in both armies: grandfathers, fathers-in-law, uncles, brothers, sons, grandsons, cousins, teachers, friends, and beloved companions. Among them were maternal uncles, fathers-in-law, grandnephews, and other revered elders. He saw many of his kinsmen in both armies facing each other, ready for battle. Witnessing all his kinsmen present there, arrayed for combat, Arjuna was overcome with deep compassion and despair *(Arjuna Vishada Yoga: 24-27)*

Commentary:

Veil of Affection Amidst Harbingers of War

Upon Arjuna's request, Krishna steered their resplendent chariot and placed it right between the Kauravas and Pandavas forces, thus raising the curtains on the catastrophic imminence of the Mahabharata war. The divine charioteer positioned the chariot directly in front of the venerable Bhishma and revered Drona—towering figures of nobility and mentors of yore. Their stern faces, once the epitome of warmth and wisdom, were now smeared with serious apprehension and veiled the earlier tender familial bonds with a mantle of stoic duty.

Bringing the chariot's clattering wheels to a halt, the soft but resolute voice of Krishna instructed the valiant prince to observe the formations before him. His words were sparse but laden with a clear directive: "Behold, O Arjuna, the assembled Kurus." These were the only words Krishna spoke in this chapter, but they became the precursor to a profound spiritual discourse that would echo through the annals of time.

Arjuna beheld the faces of grandfathers, fathers-in-law, uncles, brothers, sons, grandsons, cousins, teachers, friends, and comrades dotting the battlefront—all of whom had been integral to his life's journey. They now stood separated by the ephemeral lines of *Dharma,* ready to lock horns in a war that hummed the melancholy hymn of sacrificial duty.

Each familiar face, which reminded him of shared laughter, tears, love, and camaraderie, now shattered his spirit as he awakened to the reality of the inevitable fate that awaited all of them. His heart trembled at the thought of his arrows piercing the hearts that harbored nothing but love and affection for him. Unbridled emotions surged through Arjuna, flooding his heart with the fury of a stormy sea. The sight before him unsettled his previously resolute intellect. The haunting echo of inevitable loss and sorrow ripped through the chambers of his heart, threatening to plunge his warrior spirit into a depth of despondency.

Turbulent Thoughts: The Perilous Path of a Perturbed Mind

Because the Bhagavad Gita openly challenges the unrest that enveloped Arjuna and his hesitation to take up arms on the brink of war, it is often misinterpreted as a narrative that advocates conflict over retreat. However, within the profundity of this perplexing dialogue lies a more serious exploration into human psychology and the quintessence of *Dharma.* The melancholy that overcame Arjuna was a manifestation of an emotional turbulence rooted in binding attachment (*Raga)* and aversion (*Dvesha*), loud enough to momentarily drown the raging clamor of the battlefield around him. On closer inspection, the crippling despair in Arjuna's heart mirrors humanity's pervasive struggle in the face of emotionally charged situations that confuse its sense of duty.

A mother's instinctive love that stands strong to defend her child's wrong or a doctor's decisive pause at the threshold of life and death illustrate how human emotions can obscure or illuminate the path of *Dharma,* or righteous duty. We are often tossed about by the fleeting waves of likes and dislikes that ruffle our power of discernment and keep us from doing what ought to be done. Through Arjuna's crisis, the Bhagavad Gita sheds light on this intrinsic human frailty.

The enlightening dialogue on the battlefield of Kurukshetra goes beyond merely being a debate of war versus peace. It scrutinizes the essence of decision-making, action, and the pursuit of righteousness amid overwhelming cries of personal emotions and biases. The whispers of *Dharma* are often consumed by the assertive cries of *Raga* and *Dvesha.* The Bhagavad Gita stresses the importance of a discerning and resilient mind despite any emotional upheavals it encounters.

The Gita emphasizes mastery over one's emotions and helps strengthen the ability to perform one's duty without personal biases, thus paving the way toward righteous action. It is not the external circumstances but the hesitant nature of our minds, shackled by the chains of attachment and aversion, that lead us astray from *Dharma,* explains the Gita. Arjuna's chariot, poised between the two armies, symbolizes the crossroads we all encounter, where the confusion between emotions and duty frays the fibers of our resolve.

Krishna's discourse in the Bhagavad Gita does not provoke Arjuna to war; it steers him toward clarity and urges him to rise above the mire of binding likes and dislikes and courageously respond to the call of *Dharma.* It explains to humanity that only in the still waters of a balanced mind can one behold the clear reflection of righteous action, free from the distortions of emotional turmoil.

The Kurukshetra battlefield vividly portrays humanity's emotional struggles in the pursuit of righteousness. The following *shlokas* will more explicitly reveal this fundamental human predicament through a thorough dissection of Arjuna's dilemma. They will help us understand the overwhelming influence of *Raga* (binding attachment) and *Dvesha* (aversion) on our judgment and actions.

The Wakeful Warrior's Waver: The Paradox of Gudakesha

The Sanskrit name *Gudakesha,* used here to address Arjuna, originates from two words: *Guda,* meaning 'sleep,' and *Isha,* meaning 'lord' or 'master.' Therefore, Gudakesha translates as 'master or conqueror of sleep.' This title glorifies Arjuna's persistent spirit and unwavering dedication, which even cast aside sleep in pursuit of duty. His character embodies the essence of relentless effort and a ceaseless quest for excellence.

However, even a stalwart like Arjuna found himself completely disoriented amidst the exacting demands of the Kurukshetra battlefield. His plight reiterates that our journey through the mysterious terrains of mortal existence demands more than mere worldly wisdom or corporeal prowess. Even the seasoned, disciplined warrior in Arjuna cowered before the turbulent tempests of emotional turmoil, illustrating the necessity of inner, spiritual armor to combat life's difficulties.

Dearest Demons: The Silent Struggle of Self-Control

These *shlokas* illuminate the resounding battle within each of us. Being portrayed as the emblem of self-control, Arjuna is shown to possess a poised might capable of vanquishing the relentless tirade of *adharmic* (unrighteous) impulses infesting the unexplored crevices of the human psyche. His decisive intent to annihilate these threatening forces aligns with the enduring power of self-mastery.

However, the crusade of self-regulation reveals itself as a formidable task when faced with harsh reality. An embodiment of spiritual wisdom and discernment, the divine charioteer strategically places self-control face-to-face with the daunting array of unhealthy thoughts and emotions. This is the first step toward vigilant monitoring, as it sheds light on the foes disguised as cherished emotions and hardened beliefs lurking within.

We stand stunned, realizing that these mysterious foes are not external entities but intimate fragments of our personas. The deadly threads of lust, ego, ingrained habits, and errant emotions, woven intricately into the fabric of our identity, present a harrowing vista. The deeply embedded *adharmic* forces, nurtured and fortified by familial influences, societal norms, and personal misinterpretations, embody a deceptive charm, binding the Spirit in a tangle of delusion.

Herein lies the profound paradox: self-sabotaging tendencies so closely intertwined with one's self-identity leave us utterly perplexed. One's yearning for liberation battles the fear of losing one's perceived self, just as it unleashed a fierce storm of confusion within *Gudakesha*, the conqueror of sleep, now seemingly caught in confounding wakefulness.

Arjuna's hesitance represents the tug-of-war between self-control and the peculiar hold of ingrained negativities. His battle resonates with the spiritual struggle of every earnest seeker on a perennial quest for self-mastery through the impenetrable veils of ignorance.

The objective commentary of these *shlokas* expounds on Arjuna's predicament at the onset of a bloody war against his own kith and kin. The vivid imagery displays the inner turmoil caused by the violent clash of familial bonds and moral duty. By sketching a warrior's poignant hesitation at the brink of a historic war, it dramatically illustrates the persistent discord between personal affiliations and the righteous path of *Dharma*.

Subjectively, these *shlokas* explore the symbolic representation of the internal battlefield by portraying Arjuna as the epitome of self-control against pervasive *adharmic* forces within. They illuminate the demanding journey of self-mastery despite the blinding lure of ingrained negativities that resemble the quintessential struggle of every earnest seeker to break free from self-created delusions and attain Self-Realization. By familiarizing us with Arjuna's battle, these *shlokas* encourage us to investigate the uncharted territories of our inner self and align our innate instincts with the sublime essence of *Dharma*.

"Often disguised as nobility, decisions birthed from a weakened mind carry the seeds of peril."

Shlokas 28, 29, 30 & 31: From Kurukshetra to the Core: Unfurling of Inner Struggles

कृपया परयाऽऽविष्टः विषीदन्निदमब्रवीत् ।
अर्जुन उवाच -
दृष्ट्वेमं स्वजनं कृष्ण युयुत्सुं समुपस्थितम् ||28||

सीदन्ति मम गात्राणि मुखं च परिशुष्यति ।
वेपथुश्च शरीरे मे रोमहर्षश्च जायते ||29||

गाण्डीवं स्रंसते हस्तात् त्व क्चैव परिदह्यते ।
न च शक्नोम्यवस्थातुं भ्रमतीव च मे मनः ||30||

निमित्तानि च पश्यामि विपरीतानि केशव ।
न च श्रेयोऽनुपश्यामि हत्वा स्वजनमाहवे ||31||

kṛpayā parayā"viṣṭaḥ viṣīdannidamabravīt |
arjuna uvāca -
dṛṣṭvēmaṁ svajanaṁ kṛṣṇa yuyutsuṁ samupasthitam ||28||

sīdanti mama gātrāṇi mukhaṁ ca pariśuṣyati |
vēpathuśca śarīrē mē rōmaharṣaśca jāyatē ||29||

gāṇḍīvaṁ sraṁsatē hastāt tvakcaiva paridahyatē |
na ca śaknōmyavasthātuṁ bhramatīva ca mē manaḥ ||30||

nimittāni ca paśyāmi viparītāni kēśava |
na ca śrēyō'nupaśyāmi hatvā svajanamāhavē ||31||

Translation:

"Overwhelmed with profound compassion and sinking into despair upon beholding his very own arrayed in battle, Arjuna spoke:

"O Krishna, as I see my kin poised for battle, a shudder runs through my body, and my mouth dries up. I tremble as the hair on my body stands on end. My bow, the instrument of action, slips from my grasp, and my skin seems aflame. I cannot stand firm as my mind whirls in turmoil. Inauspicious omens cloud my sight, O Keshava, and I see no merit in slaying my kith in this battle. Victory, kingdom, and pleasures seem to lose their allure in this hour of dread." *(Arjuna Vishada Yoga:* 28-31*)*

Commentary:

From Quiver to Quavering: Arjuna's Inner Battlefield

Arjuna's unfolding crisis mirrors the intrinsic human struggle when faced with daunting challenges. We are chained, as it were, by our deep-seated binding attachments (*Raga*) and aversions (*Dvesha*). A ripple of distress (*Shoka*) courses through our psyche when life's scenarios provoke these latent bindings. It turns into a storm of disruptive emotions that eventually throws a veil of delusion (*Moha*) over our innate wisdom and sends us hurtling into complete disarray.

Arjuna, an otherwise valiant warrior, personifies this classic human struggle. Arjuna's heart quivered on hearing the clarion call of war, not at the sight of the formidable foe arrayed before him but due to emotional storms roiling his mind. The once-clear demarcation of *Dharma* (duty) and *adharma* (unrighteousness) began to blur. Up until this moment, Arjuna was convinced he had to fight and conquer these extraordinary personalities who stood by the unrighteous. But when it came to action, he was suddenly crippled by the tender bonds of kinship (*Svajanam*) that began pulling at the strings of his heart.

Arjuna here is not exhibiting the selfless love embodied by enlightened souls like Buddha. His feelings are the outcome of binding attachment. The devastating attachments he nurtured for his kith and kin expanded into an overwhelming fog of delusion that completely obscured the path of duty before him. The once steady hands that wielded the mighty *Gandiva* bow now trembled, exposing the fierce storm that raged within.

The negative omens (*Nimita*) perceived by Arjuna confirm his fall into a chasm of despair. His internal conflict does not brood the moral dilemma posed by the battlefield but sheds light on the shackles of attachment and consequent sorrow that ensnare a mighty spirit disconnected from the grace of *Dharma*. The Mahabharata war is not merely a tale of valor. It dramatically portrays how even the most robust can tremble before the phantoms of attachment and aversion.

Keshava: Queller of Inner Demons

As Arjuna finds himself trapped in the entangling vines of doubt and sorrow, he invokes Krishna as Keshava, a guiding light through the darkness of internal conflict. Keshava, as delineated in the sacred *Vishnu Sahasranama*, has various insightful interpretations, each providing nuance to Arjuna's cry for clarity at the brink of the imminent war. One meaning of Keshava is 'He who possesses beautiful locks of hair,' glorifying the divine charm and grace that Krishna exudes. Keshava also means 'Vanquisher of the demon *Keshi*,' symbolically translating as 'He who eradicates beastly tendencies within.'

Arjuna trembles with despair in the throes of the impending battle, where blood ties are bound to clash in the jaws of death. The anxiety of destroying his loved ones bites at his warrior resolve, seeding doubt in the heart that once braved many a battle. Here, the utterance of Keshava is a potent reminder of the dominion of Divine Power over adversity. The name invokes grace, as it were, for liberation from the inner demons that bind the mind to ignorance and delusion.

Moreover, *Keshava's* etymology further highlights the unity of Brahma (*Ka*) and Shiva (*Isha*), symbolizing the harmonious confluence of creation and destruction, a prelude to the cosmic dance that is about to unfold on the battlefield of Kurukshetra. The invocation of Krishna as Keshava is an ardent plea for divine intervention to sever the chains of attachment and ignorance that shackle Arjuna. It signals the beginning of a profound discourse that will forever illuminate the path of righteousness through the darkness of despair.

Arjuna subtly acknowledges that divine intercession is necessary to navigate through the tempest of his moral dilemma by calling out to Keshava. Each syllable of Keshava is a cry for triumph over the tormenting discord between duty and attachment. It begs the divine charioteer to steer the overwhelmed warrior through the fog of delusion toward the dawn of discerning wisdom.

These *shlokas* go way beyond the context of the Kurukshetra war and onto the grander battlefield within each mind. They chalk out a path for humanity to travel from entangled emotions to the enlightened realm of wisdom. By describing Arjuna's emotional upheaval, the Bhagavad Gita sheds light on the eternal battle waged within the depths of every human heart, making its teachings as relevant today as they were in Arjuna's time.

Harmonics of Inner Dissonance: Arjuna's Silent Symphony of Struggle

By minutely analyzing the Mahabharata's traditional battlefield and relating it to the raging battle within, these *shlokas* take us through the unknown alleys of the human psyche.

On the battlefield of Kurukshetra, the soliloquy of Arjuna's inner discourse reveals a warrior's dilemma and makes us aware of the ceaseless tussle between self-control and untamed emotions that torment us. These poignant *shlokas do* not merely describe a fleeting moment of a warrior's vulnerability but encapsulate the essence of every human's struggle when faced with distressing situations.

These *shlokas* vividly illustrate the utter failure of self-control in the face of deeply ingrained fears, attachments, and aversions. This helpless resignation by body and mind is the truth of the havoc played by unmanaged emotions and thoughts. Arjuna's trembling form, parched throat, and failing strength symbolize the physical manifestation of mental disquiet. When a tempest of destructive emotions is unleashed, the physiological manifestations can range from gnawing anxiety rattling the core to overwhelming hopelessness that entirely steals one's joy of living.

The metaphor also exposes the shackles that bind us to our habitual negative thoughts and cravings. When faced with a troubling scenario, a torrent of conflicting emotions gush through the mind's corridors, making a stalwart like Arjuna's convictions waver on the battlefield by veiling his discernment with a fog of despair.

Modern neuroscience explains how a perceived threat can send our emotional brain into a whirl, eclipsing the rational mind and plunging us into a fight-flight or freeze response, like Arjuna's plight. His emotional turmoil—an amalgam of compassion, fear, and attachment—eclipsed his *Dharma as a* warrior and thrust him into a state of utter despair.

In conclusion, Arjuna's condition on the battlefield of Kurukshetra is similar to the internal battles we face. These *shlokas* unravel the difficulty of self-control amidst relentless desires, fears, and attachments. They shed light on the fragile human condition yet whisper a promise of transcendence if guided by wisdom and a more discerning intellect. By vividly describing Arjuna's dilemma, they encourage us to venture inward, confront and quell our inner storms, and unearth a wellspring of clarity and equanimity in and through life's ongoing battles.

> *"The true battle is fought not upon the field of Kurukshetra, but within the unfathomable depths of our minds where fear and courage fight for dominance under the floodlight of consciousness."*

Shlokas 32, 33, 34, 35, 36 & 37: Arjuna's Aversion: The Excuse Dance on *Dharma*'s War Stage

न काङ्क्षे विजयं कृष्ण न च राज्यं सुखानि च ।
किं नो राज्येन गोविन्द किं भोगैर्जीवितेन वा ||32||

येषामर्थे काङ्क्षितं नः राज्यं भोगाः सुखानि च ।
त इमेऽवस्थिता युद्धे प्राणांस्त्यक्त्वा धनानि च ||33||

आचार्याः पितरः पुत्राः तथैव च पितामहाः ।
मातुलाः श्वशुराः पौत्राः श्यालाः सम्बन्धिनस्तथा ||34||

एतान्न हन्तुमिच्छामि घ्नतोऽपि मधुसूदन |
अपि त्रैलोक्यराज्यस्य हेतोः किं नु महीकृते ||35||

निहत्य धार्तराष्ट्रान्नः का प्रीतिः स्याज्जनार्दन |
पापमेवाश्रयेदस्मान् हत्वैतानाततायिनः ||36||

तस्मान्नार्हा वयं हन्तुं धार्तराष्ट्रान्स्वबान्धवान् |
स्वजनं हि कथं हत्वा सुखिनः स्याम माधव ||37||

na kāṅkṣē vijayaṁ kṛṣṇa na ca rājyaṁ sukhāni ca |
kiṁ nō rājyēna gōvinda kiṁ bhōgairjīvitēna vā ||32||

yēṣāmarthē kāṅkṣitaṁ naḥ rājyaṁ bhōgāḥ sukhāni ca |
ta imē'vasthitā yuddhē prāṇāṁstyaktvā dhanāni ca ||33||

ācāryāḥ pitaraḥ putrāḥ tathaiva ca pitāmahāḥ |
mātulāḥ śvaśurāḥ pautrāḥ śyālāḥ sambandhinastathā ||34||

ētānna hantumicchāmi ghnatō›pi madhusūdana |
api trailōkyarājyasya hētōḥ kiṁ nu mahīkṛtē ||35||

nihatya dhārtarāṣṭrānnaḥ kā prītiḥ syājjanārdana |
pāpamēvāśrayēdasmān hatvaitānātatāyinaḥ ||36||

tasmānnārhā vayaṁ hantuṁ dhārtarāṣṭrānsvabāndhavān |
svajanaṁ hi kathaṁ hatvā sukhinaḥ syāma mādhava ||37||

Translation:

"O Krishna, I harbor no desires for victory, kingdom, or earthly pleasures. What worth holds a kingdom, enjoyment, or even life, O Govinda? All those we seek kingdom, enjoyment, and pleasures for stand here ready for battle, having forsaken life and wealth. I have no desire to slay them, even if they are ready to slay us. Not for dominion over the three worlds, let alone this earth, would I wish to kill the sons of Dhritarashtra, O Madhusudana. O Janardana, how could we find pleasure in slaying the sons of Dhritarashtra? By committing such an act, we would only invite sin upon ourselves. Therefore, it is not fitting for us to kill the sons of Dhritarashtra, our own kin. How could we find happiness in such a deed, O Madhava?" *(Arjuna Vishada Yoga:32-37)*

Commentary:

On the battlefield of Kurukshetra, typical human emotions weaken Arjuna's mind, manifesting themselves as a torrent of despair and delusion. As seen in the preceding *shlokas*, the force of *Raga* (binding attachment) unleashed a storm of *Shoka* (emotional overwhelm) within him. He was caught in a whirlwind of confusion that incapacitated his mind and body. These *shlokas* animate Arjuna's internal turmoil, revealing how *Moha* (delusion) veils any discerning faculty.

Arjuna finds himself caught in the juncture of having to choose between personal sentiments and the directives of *Dharma*. In a desperate attempt to rationalize his reluctance, Arjuna crafts arguments that prima facie appear rational and morally upright. He proclaims his utter disregard for victory, pleasures, or the grandeur of kingdoms. He wonders aloud about the essence of an empire, enjoyment, or even life when those he holds dear stand poised at the opposite end of his bow. His words echo the conflict many a heart faces when standing at the crossroads of duty and personal propensities.

Though disguised as righteousness, Arjuna's appeals to abandon the battlefield unwittingly swim in the tumultuous waters of emotional difficulty. The fear of losing loved ones, the despair over the imagined impacts of warfare, and the envisioned dread of familial bloodshed all rise from an abyss of emotional delusion that clouds Arjuna's judgment. His emotionally charged arguments are bereft of the essence of *Dharma*, which forever is supposed to guide one's actions.

It is essential to clarify here that the Bhagavad Gita does not contest the legitimacy of Arjuna's arguments. Instead, it peels back the layers of emotional discord to reveal his mind's instability and weakness. The Gita guides Arjuna, and through him all of humanity, to recognize that the essence of decision-making, especially when confronted with a moral dilemma, should be made by an intellect rooted in *Dharma*, not by a mind that is swayed by ephemeral emotions or fallible logic.

The Bhagavad Gita is often misinterpreted as a war-mongering text. These misinterpretations stem from an exclusive consideration of Arjuna's emotional arguments without referring to the entire context of the Mahabharata storyline.

The Bhagavad Gita does not champion war. It advocates for decisions to be made from a robust, Dharmic mindset rather than a weak, deluded one. Arjuna's circumstance serves as a profound metaphor that urges us to free ourselves from the shackles of emotional delusion and seek the clarity of *Dharma*, especially when the heart trembles in the face of duty.

We witness Arjuna, the mighty warrior, turn into a mere mortal debilitated by love, fear, and delusion. His arguments seem noble but diverge from the path of *Dharma*. It is a pivotal moment that prompts the discourse of the Bhagavad Gita. It exposes our inner Kurukshetra and urges us to seek a sanctuary of wisdom amidst the tempest of life's moral and emotional conflicts.

Sketches of Strength: The Self-Control Struggle Within Temptations' Turmoil

These *shlokas* bring to life the tumultuous battlefield of the human psyche, where self-control is acutely tested amidst the relentless onslaught of destructive emotions and unhealthy thought patterns. The dismantling of Arjuna's usually unshakable resolve symbolizes self-control, faced with the daunting task of quelling the tempest of inner demons. His internal crisis resembles humanity's difficulty in choosing immediate gratifications, represented by the relatives and kinsfolk in these *shlokas*, or adhering to the higher wisdom that beseeches cessation of such indulgences.

The narrative displays the myriad excuses our self-control conjures up in the face of temptations and challenges. The battle against the vagaries of our unrestrained mind is not easy; it is a grueling war. By vividly portraying Arjuna's plight, these *shlokas* expose the mind's convoluted rationale as it argues against abandoning known pleasures for unknown virtuous rewards. Even the thought of relinquishing familiar yet detrimental habits breeds fear of altering one's core personality or draining the charm of existence.

A profound insight shared by modern psychology reinforces this narrative. When one identifies with negative emotional states, the reins of control slip away, entangling the individual in a vicious cycle of self-sabotage. One's identity morphs into a fortress for these negative emotions, defending them against the intervention of self-control.

The Buddhist scripture Dhammapada also describes this eternal struggle through Mara, the symbol of unwholesome impulses. Mara's allure is powerful. His illusions distort reality, plunging the self into the depth of ignorance. Overcoming Mara is symbolic of conquering one's vices. It is the ideal of self-control that Arjuna must muster to override the tide of despondency.

As seen earlier, through the story of Adam and Eve, The Holy Bible also highlights the human propensity to succumb to temptations. The serpent's crafty persuasion represents the magnetic allure of negative tendencies that rock humanity's self-control. The veil of innocence lifted as the apple was plucked mirrors the precarious edge on which self-control teeters.

These *shlokas,* aligned with modern psychology, Buddhist teachings, and Biblical narratives, reiterate tenets of timeless wisdom. They encourage a relentless pursuit to break free of the shackles of transient gratifications and establish oneself in keen understanding and eternal serenity. Arjuna's hesitance mirrors the endless confusion wreaking havoc within the heart of humanity.

Radiance in Names: Unfurling the Divinity of Krishna in the Kurukshetra Dialogue

These thought-provoking *shlokas* from Chapter 1 of the Bhagavad Gita carry a melodic resonance of divine epithets, each profoundly meaningful. The names ascribed to Krishna in these *shlokas* guide Arjuna—and humanity—toward a deeper understanding of the Divine.

Madhusudhana: The Divine Disbander of Delusive Desires

Madhusudhana is derived from the Sanskrit roots - *Madhu*, which means 'sweet but binding attachments' akin to honey, and Sudhana, which translates as 'the vanquisher.' Hence, *Madhusudhana* means the one who overcomes the bonds of attachment. Arjuna, weakened by his overwhelming affections, desperately needs to identify with what *Madhusudhana* represents.

By invoking Krishna with this name, he acknowledges the bonds clouding his discernment and seeks liberation to see through the delusion that confuses his duty.

Janardhana: The Cosmic Arbiter of Karmic Justice

Janardhana finds its roots in *Jana*, meaning 'people,' and *Ardhana*, meaning to 'punish or reward.' It embodies the principle of cosmic reciprocity—rewarding virtue and admonishing vice. As Janardhana, Krishna symbolizes the unyielding law of *Karma*. Arjuna's invocation of Krishna as Janardhana alludes to the karmic crossroads faced by every being on the battlefield of *Dharma*. It urges a deeper inquiry into what is righteous beyond transient emotional waves.

Janardhana also means the 'protector of people.' Teachers of Vedanta elucidate the two-sided plea of Arjuna through this invocation so beautifully. On one hand, Arjuna expresses his confusion as to why He, who is revered as a 'protector of people', is engaging him in this gory act of killing his loved ones. And on the other hand, he is seeking *Bhagavan*

Shri Krishna's protection and guidance through this heartbreaking ordeal.

Govinda: The Multifaceted Guardian

The name Govinda blossoms like a budding lotus in the heart of every earnest spiritual seeker, each petal an acknowledgment of divine guardianship and profound wisdom. *Govinda* delicately couples *Go* and *Vinda*, encompassing the earth, cows, speech, and Vedas. As the Earth cradles all life, Govinda emerges as the cosmic custodian, ensuring the rhythmic flow of existence. This name, when invoked, transports a seeker into a divine sanctuary where *Dharma* echoes as the living, breathing ethos of existence.

The portrayal of Govinda as a cowherd goes beyond its literal depiction and represents a higher play of spiritual stewardship. Guarding cows is emblematic of purity and sustenance. Just as a cowherd leads cows to graze only on the greenest of pastures, similarly, Govinda leads us from the physical to the subtle, urging our primal instincts to align with higher wisdom.

Govinda reverberates within speech and the Vedas as the silent core from which eternal wisdom emanates. Krishna, as Govinda, is not just a character in a storyline but the voice of the scriptures, a whisper from the heart of the sages. As Arjuna grapples with the shadows of misconceptions, invoking Govinda shows his deep yearning for divine intervention that aligns the transient with the eternal. He is pleading, as it were, for the lost at heart to be guided into the sanctuary of ancient wisdom that is patiently waiting to be discovered by all of mankind.

Krishna: The Universal Magnet of Endless Allure

Krishna is a melody reverberating through the cosmos, humming the grand narrative of existence, consciousness, and contentment. By whispering the name Krishna, we do not merely call upon a deity but invoke a consciousness that dances through every cell of the universe. Krishna has many meanings. Derived from the Sanskrit root *Krish*, which means 'to be' or 'existence,' and *Na,* meaning 'contentment,' the name Krishna describes the essence of 'being an endless fountain of contentment.' Each syllable rings with the echo of eternity, drawing beings into the rhythmic dance of existence.

According to Vedanta, *'Sat-Chit-Ananda'* represents the essence of Supreme Reality: - Existence, Consciousness, and Unlimited Contentment. The name Krishna embodies this triune essence. As *Sat*, He is the unchanging reality. As *Chit*, He is the consciousness that illuminates, and as *Ananda*, He is the contentment that is at the very core of existence. Krishna is thus a mantra that aligns the seeker with the sublime rhythm of the cosmos.

Krishna also signifies *Akarshayati*, an element of magnetism. His irresistible allure tugs at the hearts of the weary, the joyful, the seeker, and the sage alike. This name embodies a celestial magnetism that magnetizes all beings toward the core of ultimate joy.

The name also holds a visual essence: *Krishna Varnayati*, depicted with a dark complexion, symbolizes an encompassing presence that absorbs all into itself. This dark hue is not a mere color but suggests a depth that holds the mysteries of existence within it.

The name Krishna encapsulates everything from the depths of ancient wisdom to the heart of contemporary human longing. It is an invocation that transcends time, passing through the dense forests of Vrindavan to the battlefield of Kurukshetra and further into the heart of every soul that seeks to understand the enigma of existence. The mere utterance of Krishna is an invitation to dive into a boundless ocean of love and wisdom. It is a peek into the divine play, a pathway to the transcendent realm of Self-Realization. Contemplating this name, one partakes in the divine romance between the finite and the infinite and is beckoned to step into the limitless horizon, where one's heartbeats resonate with the ageless melody of Krishna. Arjuna's invocation of Krishna is a soulful yearning for reconnection to this celestial harmony as he seeks solace and guidance amidst the storms of despair and moral dilemmas.

The unfolding of these divine epithets in the heart of Kurukshetra's turmoil opens a spiritual lexicon. Each name of Krishna carries a world of wisdom. The etymological explorations of these names pave a path for deeper meditative insights, guiding every earnest seeker toward a richer understanding of life's divine play. Each name becomes a meditative mantra, unveiling layers of ethereal wisdom and leading the seeker closer to the heart of existence.

"Living a life of self-control is akin to walking on a tightrope, with relentless gusts of temptations attempting to sway the balance of the steadfast mind."

Shlokas 38 & 39: Family or Foe: Arjuna's Pivotal Predicament

यद्यप्येते न पश्यन्ति लोभोपहतचेतसः |
कुलक्षयकृतं दोषं मित्रद्रोहे च पातकम् ||38||

कथं न ज्ञेयमस्माभिः पापादस्मान्निवर्तितुम् |
कुलक्षयकृतं दोषं प्रपश्यद्भिर्जनार्दन ||39||

yadyapyētē na paśyanti lōbhōpahatacētasaḥ |
kulakṣayakr̥taṁ dōṣaṁ mitradrōhē ca pātakam ||*38*||

kathaṁ na jñēyamasmābhiḥ pāpādasmānnivartitum |
kulakṣayakr̥taṁ dōṣaṁ prapaśyadbhirjanārdana ||*39*||

Translation:

"Even though these (Kauravas), with minds overpowered by greed, see no wrong in destroying a family and betraying a friend, we (Pandavas), who see the sin in destroying a family, should turn away from this evil. How could we, O Janardana, knowingly commit this sin of destruction, seeing clearly as we do the wrong that accrues from the downfall of a family?" *(Arjuna Vishada Yoga: 38-39)*

Commentary:

Unveiling the Delusion: The Futility of Valid Arguments from a Troubled Psyche

Delving deeper into Arjuna's moral tangle, we unearth subtle emotions and vehement justifications that vividly paint a dramatic scenario of *Adharma* pitched against *Dharma*, carrying the hue of existential melancholy. These *shlokas* set the floodlights upon a mind caught in the tempest of worldly attachments, bringing into focus a central facet of the cycle of *Samsara*, where *Raga* (binding attachment) morphs into *Shoka* (emotional overwhelm) and culminates in *Moha* (delusion).

Arjuna, echoing the voice of discernment, highlights the blindness that greed has bestowed upon the Kauravas, rendering them incapable of perceiving the mistake of destroying familial bonds and breeding hostility among kindred spirits. However, unlike the Kauravas, Arjuna and his forces are not blindfolded by greed; their vision pierces through the fog of ignorance, sensing the impending calamity that would befall the familial and social fabric with the clashing of blood against blood on the battlefield. His words carry moral wisdom and reiterate the atrocity of family destruction and betrayal of friends, an evil the Kauravas are blind to. On the other hand, the Pandavas find themselves caught in a moral dilemma despite the evil that stands gaping at them.

This stirring monologue is, in reality, an unbelievable guise of self-deception. Arjuna's reason for withdrawing from the battle, though backed by sound moral rationale, originates from a mind incapacitated by emotional turmoil and existential dread. His plea discloses a desperate need for validation from Krishna to escape from this distressing duty that *Dharma* mandates. But the stoic silence of the Divine charioteer Krishna symbolizes transcendental wisdom that awaits its unfurling at the right moment of receptivity.

The moral and emotional dilemma Arjuna struggles with illustrates the formidable power of the mind in concocting impeccable arguments to abstain from one's duty. Each justification, each plea, mirrors a mind striving to escape the trial of *Dharma*, thereby keeping the endless cycle of Samsara active. The validity of Arjuna's arguments is undeniable. An eruption from a weak and deluded mind renders them out of context. They highlight the profound challenge of upholding *Dharma* amidst the turmoil of human emotions and worldly attachments.

Through Arjuna's weakened stance on the battlefield, we are urged to delve deeper into the eternal dialogue between duty and desire, righteousness, and the moral dilemma that transpires within us. These *shlokas* reflect the perennial human struggle to transcend the self-imposed shackles of *Moha* (delusion) and implore us to seek the righteous path with a mind unclouded by transient emotions. For at every bend and crossroad of life, we are tested for our alignment with *Dharma*.

Arjuna's plight journeys us, as it were, through the core of human existence, with each word of Arjuna and the reciprocated silence of Krishna animating the essential struggle and eventual transcendence of the human mind.

The Inner Conundrum: When Logic Entwines with Emotion

These *shlokas* transport us from the rugged battlefield of Kurukshetra to the complex puzzle within our minds. The idea of Self-Control, personified by Arjuna, is challenged by an onslaught of alternating logic and emotion. Every argument directed by the ego sheds light upon the moral and ethical dilemmas confronting the self.

Self-control acknowledges the paradoxical nature of existence. Harmful emotions and thoughts, though detrimental, form the fabric of our internal cosmos, the 'family' of our being. This recognition, though enlightening, leads to a pacifist tendency, a reluctance to engage in internal warfare for fear of destroying the very essence that constitutes 'me.'

Let us understand this with a familiar scenario—a resolve to overcome procrastination. When the mind embarks on this quest, it instantaneously confronts a battalion of comforting excuses. Like seasoned politicians, habitual tendencies present a valid case for temporary indulgence, promising reform at a future convenience. Yet, as time exposes the underlying self-deceit, the stark reality of lost opportunities and dwindling time hits hard.

The Bhagavad Gita gently introduces us to the deceptive charm of unhealthy emotions that, over time, nestle within our psyche as endearing companions. This idea resonates with Lord Buddha's insights on the mental tremors that ensue when one endeavors to liberate oneself from the clutches of evil realms. Even Biblical scriptures echo this sentiment and warn against the difficult journey of a double-minded individual tossed in the storm of transient desires, marching toward ruin.

These *shlokas* encourage us to navigate through emotional turmoil with discernment. They highlight the imperativeness of confronting and overcoming internal adversaries to attain inner equanimity and true self-mastery. Through this allegorical journey, the *shlokas* not only elucidate the transient nature of emotional attachments but help us break free of delusion and lead us toward a dawn of Self-Realization.

"Unhealthy thoughts and emotions often receive a warm defense in the courtroom of the mind, making them appear less like intruders and more like family."

Shlokas 40, 41, 42, 43 & 44: Arjuna's Woven Rationalizations: Deluded Visions, Crafted Justifications

कुलक्षये प्रणश्यन्ति कुलधर्माः सनातनाः |
धर्मे नष्टे कुलं कृत्स्नम् अधर्मोऽभिभवत्युत ||40||

अधर्माभिभवात्कृष्ण प्रदुष्यन्ति कुलस्त्रियः |
स्त्रीषु दुष्टासु वार्ष्णेय जायते वर्णसङ्करः ||41||

सङ्करो नरकायैव कुलघ्नानां कुलस्य च ।
पतन्ति पितरो ह्येषां लुप्तपिण्डोदकक्रियाः ||42||

दोषैरेतैः कुलघ्नानां वर्णसङ्करकारकैः ।
उत्साद्यन्ते जातिधर्माः कुलधर्माश्च शाश्वताः ||43||

उत्सन्नकुलधर्माणां मनुष्याणां जनार्दन ।
नरकेऽनियतं वासः भवतीत्यनुशुश्रुम ||44||

kulakṣayē praṇaśyanti kuladharmāḥ sanātanāḥ |
dharmē naṣṭē kulaṁ kṛtsnam adharmō'bhibhavatyuta ||*40*||

adharmābhibhavātkṛṣṇa praduṣyanti kulastriyaḥ |
strīṣu duṣṭāsu vārṣṇēya jāyatē varṇasaṅkaraḥ ||*41*||

saṅkarō narakāyaiva kulaghnānāṁ kulasya ca |
patanti pitarō hyēṣāṁ luptapiṇḍōdakakriyāḥ ||*42*||

dōṣairētaiḥ kulaghnānāṁ varṇasaṅkarakārakaiḥ |
utsādyantē jātidharmāḥ kuladharmāśca śāśvatāḥ ||*43*||

utsannakuladharmāṇāṁ manuṣyāṇāṁ janārdana |
narakē'niyataṁ vāsaḥ bhavatītyanuśuśruma ||*44*||

Translation:

"With the end of the family, its ancient traditions perish. When these traditions are lost, disorder overcomes the entire family. O Krishna, with the prevalence of lawlessness, the women of the family become immoral, and with the corruption of womanhood arises a confusion of progeny. This confusion leads the family and the family destroyers to hellish states, for their ancestors fall, deprived of the ceremonies of offerings and water. By these wrongdoings of the family destroyers, who cause confusion of lineages, the eternal duties of the family and the timeless laws are obliterated. O Janardana, we have heard that dwelling in hell is inevitable for those whose family duties have been shattered due to the loss of traditions." *(Arjuna Vishada Yoga: 40-44)*

Commentary:

These *shlokas* continue to paint Arjuna's inner tussle in the face of the impending war. Here, we witness the brilliant yet distressed archer belting out a flurry of incoherent rationalizations in a desperate effort to align with *Dharma* despite the stark realities of war. Arjuna stands wholly incapacitated by *Shoka* (sorrow) due to *Moha* (delusion) that is brought about by *Raga* (binding attachments). His thinking capacity is totally eclipsed by the darkness that keeps out the luminescent essence of *Dharma.*

Arjuna voices a legitimate concern about destroying familial bonds and the societal upheaval such a war would precipitate. The aftermath of such a terrible war threatens to erode the very bedrock of society, disintegrating family units and consequently leading to a derangement of social order. *Varna Sankara's* metaphor paints a vivid image of the probable chaos, where societal roles become mismatched and social order descends into a cacophony of discord.

Arjuna's warning of ancestors rejecting the ritual offerings symbolizes a disconnection from the roots of tradition and values, alluding to a cultural dissonance reverberating through the generations. The grim imagery of a 'hellish state' is highlighted to stress the moral decay and societal unrest that may follow in the wake of the war. However, amidst this overdramatized despair, it is vital to pierce through Arjuna's fear-tinged arguments to glimpse the higher *Dharma.*

Arjuna's impassioned perspective overlooks the larger context: the call for a righteous war to uphold *Dharma* and restore cosmic balance. His apprehensions prompt an involuntary reflection on the wars of the world, especially the Second World War. Had the allies shrunk back from confronting the threatening shadow of Nazi ideology, the pages of history would be scripted in a much darker ink.

In the Name of Varshneya: Arjuna's Silent Plea

The title *Varshneya* is bestowed upon Krishna in recognition of His descent from the illustrious *Vrishi* clan, highlighting the magnificence and honor of His lineage. In addressing Krishna as *Varshneya*, Arjuna subtly hints at the devastation a civil war could inflict upon the noble lineage of the Kurus. His invocation serves as a poignant reminder of the irreplaceable loss of heritage and legacy that such a conflict would bring about.

Mind's Dilemma: The Paradox of Control

Arjuna, exemplifying self-control in this scenario, presents a powerful argument: the danger of forcibly suppressing one's thoughts and emotions. Just as he contemplates the ramifications of warfare on the physical field, so does he, symbolically, contemplate the psychological terrain within.

Self-control, as these *Shlokas* illuminate, is a challenging pursuit. It often leads one to suppress thoughts deemed harmful or unhealthy. However, repressing these thoughts could be detrimental. For in forcibly quieting our minds, aren't we at risk of stifling its natural essence? There is a palpable apprehension that this mental disarmament could throw our psyche into disarray, disrupting our emotions, perceptions, and fundamental behaviors.

Like the battlefield, the mind is inhabited by many thoughts. These thoughts, akin to those of warriors, have their roles and their purposes. In our eager attempts to control them, we risk annihilating both positive and negative 'warriors' of the mind, giving birth to a new cognitive landscape marked by altered thoughts, emotions, and inclinations.

Our senses serve as gateways to the external world. Embodying the 'feminine' aspect in this narrative, they intertwine with our thoughts to shape the very fabric of our experiences. Destroy or alter the natural mental warriors, and our senses, deprived of their traditional thought partners, may find themselves orphaned. But nature abhors a vacuum.

Slowly, these senses may align with other potentially unnatural emotions or inclinations. This distorted union could radically alter our perception, casting shadows where light once was or magnifying minor elements into looming specters. An eye, unanchored by its corresponding thought, might misperceive; an ear might misconstrue, leading to misjudgments, misunderstandings, and potentially, a descent into a cognitive 'hellish' state.

Arjuna's dilemma highlighted in these *shlokas* is profound: Can the quest for inner peace and mental order, through forcible control, lead us further into chaos and estrangement from our mind's natural state? These concerns, voiced through Arjuna's rationalizations, seem valid but, as we will see, are out of context. Allowing unhealthy thoughts and emotions to reign unchecked is more dangerous. The key lies in discernment and a balanced approach to mental mastery.

In summary, Arjuna grapples with the potential devastation of war, emphasizing the erosion of familial ties and cultural values. The tug-of-war within his bosom mirrors our inner conflict: the struggle between wanting to rein in negative emotions and the concern of suppressing our true nature. Even though these are valid arguments, they must be evaluated under the magnifying lens of *Dharma*.

Beyond Distortions: Caste's Unjust Departure from *Varna*

It is crucial to pause here and address the misunderstandings that have plagued the term '*Varna*,' often wrongly conflated with 'caste.' Down the ages, a misguided notion has taken root, suggesting that one's worth is preordained by birth rather than shaped by character and deeds. Seeing such beliefs erroneously linked to *Sanatana Dharma* is distressing, as they wholly contradict its true essence and teachings. We unequivocally denounce this caste-based discrimination, which is a glaring misinterpretation of the ideals of *Sanatana Dharma*. Witnessing the prejudice stemming from such beliefs is heartbreaking, especially when *Sanatana Dharma*, at its core, champions the ideals of unity and equality.

Moreover, it is disconcerting when individuals not fully acquainted with the profound depths of *Sanatana Dharma* hastily mislabel this grand tradition based on the misguided actions of a few. It is like focusing on the fallen leaves of a vast forest and dismissing its overarching majesty. When such misconceptions are propagated from influential platforms, they fuel divisive sentiments and risk burying timeless wisdom that has been passed down the ages. We urge individuals from all levels of society to look beyond these skewed narratives and align with the authenticity of the teachings.

To reiterate with utmost clarity: The Bhagavad Gita and *Sanatana Dharma* do not endorse or support caste-based discrimination in any form. Over time, the well-intended idea of the *Varna* system has been twisted and misused, leading to caste-based discrimination. This misrepresentation is a heinous blot upon humanity's archives and warrants absolute condemnation. As we continue to unearth the gems of the Bhagavad Gita, we vow to dispel these fallacies and guide readers toward the heart of *Sanatana Dharma's* true wisdom.

Delusion crafts its own logic; a misguided mind always finds sound reason within its unsound whims.

Shlokas 45 & 46: Echoes of Regret: Arjuna's Surrender

अहो बत महत्पापं कर्तुं व्यवसिता वयम् |
यद्राज्यसुखलोभेन हन्तुं स्वजनमुद्यताः ||45||

यदि मामप्रतीकारम् अशस्त्रं शस्त्रपाणयः |
धार्तराष्ट्रा रणे हन्युः तन्मे क्षेमतरं भवेत् ||46||

ahō bata mahatpāpaṁ kartuṁ vyavasitā vayam |
yadrājyasukhalōbhēna hantuṁ svajanamudyatāḥ ||45||

yadi māmapratīkāram aśastraṁ śastrapāṇayaḥ |
dhārtarāṣṭrā raṇē hanyuḥ tanmē kṣēmataraṁ bhavēt ||46|

Translation:

"Alas, driven by our desire for royal comforts and pleasures, we stand poised to commit a grave mistake: slaying our own kin. Indeed, I would find it more preferable if the sons of Dhritarashtra, armed and ready, were to strike me down in battle while I remain unarmed and unresisting." *(Arjuna Vishada Yoga:* 45&46*)*

Frozen Amidst the Battle's Roar: The Relinquishment of Arjuna

The clamor of battle has been superseded by the deep, emotional turmoil echoing within Arjuna's heart. The fierce warrior, known for his unwavering determination, now stands paralyzed, overwhelmed in sorrow and confusion. The weight of the impending war, with its inevitable bloodshed and tragic consequences, bears heavily on his conscience.

Arjuna's voice, laden with despair, bellows: "How have we come to this?" The exclamation, *Ahō,* reveals his profound astonishment and regret. For Arjuna, the very thought of clashing swords with his own kin for the sake of a kingdom and its fleeting pleasures seems unthinkable. The word speaks to the shock of realization and the sharp sting of self-reproach.

It is evident that the charms of the throne, the allure of power and prestige, have cast a shadow over the nobler virtues of family and *Dharma*. The tragedy is not just that the Kurus are prepared for war, but that their tempting ambitions also ensnare Arjuna and the Pandavas. This thought makes him wonder: "If yes, then are we any different?"

Arjuna, in desperation, lays bare his final resolution before his charioteer Krishna, who has thus far been a silent witness. He declares he would prefer to remain unarmed, allowing the Kauravas to strike him down rather than participate in a war that would lead to the massacre of his own family. In his view, this would be a lesser crime and a more honorable end. It is a stance born from the highest principles of non-violence and self-sacrifice, highlighting the profound moral conflict gnawing at his mind.

Yet underlying Arjuna's noble sentiments is deep-seated despair and confusion. He is unable to determine the righteous path, his *swadharma*. It is not merely a choice between fighting or fleeing. In the face of overwhelming stress and emotional upheaval, Arjuna experiences a psychological freeze—not unique to him alone, but a well-documented psychological response. In high-stress situations, the human mind oscillates between the fight, flight, or freeze responses. The blare of conch shells and war cries, accentuated by his moral dilemma, has completely incapacitated Arjuna.

In these poignant verses, we glimpse a warrior at a difficult juncture, where he haplessly grapples with the profound complexities of emotions and *Dharma*. The battlefield of Kurukshetra mirrors the inner conflicts that most of us face in our lifetimes.

Whispers and Wills: The Tempted Surrender

This battle between self-control and overpowering emotions impairs every human psyche. Often, when pressure mounts and emotions get the better of us, the fortress of self-control, much like Arjuna, feels overwhelmed and thinks of relinquishing its guard.

The determined spirit, symbolized by Arjuna's steadfast nature, falters and crafts convenient arguments to justify surrender to life's many seductions. It is a psychological phenomenon humanity encounters en masse: a willful desire to uphold discipline cowers before a torrent of rationalizations. While recognizing the higher purpose of reigning in unchecked emotions and desires, self-control wrestles with uncertainty and the potential loss of immediate pleasure.

The inner dialogue is unrelenting. The self-control questions are: What assurance do I have of the promised tranquility after taming these desires? Why should I forsake the immediate gratification I derive from these sensations in the hope of elusive future contentment? There is a haunting fear of missed experiences and the belief that these emotions and temptations, being natural, are divine gifts meant to be indulged in. The reasoning concludes with a dramatic sentiment: it might be more authentic to be overwhelmed and ruined by these passions than to suppress them and risk an unnatural existence.

Be cautious here. Yielding repeatedly to fleeting desires does not satiate them; it only fuels their intensity, leading one deeper into their snare. It is akin to feeding a fire; the more you throw into it, the more it demands. Succumbing repeatedly creates a dangerous cycle of dependency, an addiction hard to break. And while the immediate attraction of these sensations is undeniable, it is vital to recognize that they seldom offer enduring happiness. Their promises are often illusory.

Like a wolf in sheep's clothing, these emotions and temptations disguise themselves as benign, even beneficial, but eventually lead the unguarded spirit astray. Wisdom is discerning the transient from the eternal, fleeting pleasures from lasting joy.

These *shlokas* vividly uncover the continuous tussle between immediate gratification and long-term contentment within the human psyche. They prompt introspection and urge one to balance the satiation of natural human desires while ever pursuing a higher, more enlightened state of being.

"Beware. Ignorance often cloaks itself in the guise of imagined wisdom."

Shloka 47: From Warrior to Wounded: Arjuna's collapse.

सञ्जय उवाच -
एवमुक्त्वाऽर्जुनः सङ्ख्ये रथोपस्थ उपाविशत् |
विसृज्य सशरं चापं शोकसंविग्नमानसः ||47||

sañjaya uvāca -
ēvamuktvā›rjunaḥ saṅkhyē rathōpastha upāviśat |
visṛjya saśaraṁ cāpaṁ śōkasaṁvignamānasaḥ ||47||

Translation:

Sanjaya narrated:

"Having spoken thus amid the battlefield, Arjuna, consumed by sorrow, cast aside his bow and arrows and, overwhelmed by distress, sank down onto his chariot." (*Arjuna Vishada Yoga*: 47)

Commentary:

The final *shloka* of this thought-provoking chapter bears witness to a poignant transformation. We watch a spirited warrior, Arjuna, renowned throughout the land for his unmatched bravery and skill. He is reduced to a weak mortal riddled with torment, his spirit trapped in the tumultuous upheaval of his emotions.

The preceding shlokas chronicle Arjuna's internal turmoil, where kinship ties mercilessly challenge the call of duty. The all-consuming power of these conflicting emotions, the paralyzing grip of attachment, and the onslaught of overwhelming sorrow culminate in a singular act: Arjuna's dropping of his famed bow, *Gandiva*, and arrows, echoing the depths of Arjuna's hopeless diffidence.

With his divine sight, Sanjaya captures this pivotal moment with vivid clarity for Dhritarashtra. Arjuna, the lion-hearted warrior, amidst the cacophony of battle cries, war drums, and blaring conch shells, finds himself silenced, not by the inescapable reality of the impending war but by the war within. His formidable weapons, once symbolic of his unwavering will, now lie discarded, mirroring the internal abandonment of his warrior identity. Seated despondently in his chariot between the two armies, he contrasts the charged atmosphere around him.

Arjuna's stance contradicts that of a strategist contemplating his next move or a warrior rallying his strength. Instead, it paints the portrait of a man defeated by his emotions, torn between social duty and personal sentiment. His emotional state raises a profound question: How does one reconcile the obligation of one's role with the essence of one's humanity? The torment created by this question paralyzes him and renders him a passive observer in the theater of life.

This concluding verse of the first chapter plunges us into Arjuna's psyche, laying bare the fragility and vulnerability that even the mightiest can experience when faced with personal dilemmas.

The Inner Retreat: Self-Control's Silent Surrender

As we have been analyzing throughout this chapter, the battlefield of Kurukshetra is a vivid allegory of the ongoing inner conflicts we grapple with. The first chapter brilliantly brings to the fore the multifaceted challenges and dilemmas innate to our very being.

The portrayal of Arjuna's vulnerability offers an evocative parallel to our intrinsic self-mastery. Just as Arjuna stands hesitant, torn between familial loyalty and *Dharma*, our self-discipline often wavers when confronted with the familiar allure of detrimental emotions and unhealthy thoughts. The seductive whispers of these feelings can be overwhelmingly persuasive, leading even the most committed to question whether it is easier to simply succumb to their might. The conclusion reached by Arjuna's heart—to abandon the fight rather than confront and subdue these inner demons—is a scenario we all struggle with in our moments of weakness.

The first chapter masterfully mirrors our internal conflicts through Arjuna's despondency. The world we perceive is a byproduct of our inner state. The world no doubt provides every stimulus. But how life ultimately plays out largely depends on how our mind processes and interprets it. It unequivocally points out that our every experience is, at its core, a mental construct.

It teaches us that if we venture into the external world without fortifying our inner selves, we risk being swayed by its vagaries. We might become susceptible, quickly taken in by the immediate gratification the world offers, even if it is at odds with our greater good. It is akin to stepping into a storm without an umbrella; we will get drenched.

Our mind is both a formidable ally and a persuasive adversary. If uncontrolled, it gives us countless justifications to indulge in our weaker impulses. Involuntarily, it tends to prioritize transient pleasures over enduring well-being.

On the surface, the culmination of Chapter One appears to be a tale of a mighty warrior paralyzed by moral and emotional turmoil on the verge of a great war. But by delving deeper, it reveals the truth of our internal battles. It is a testament to the age-old adage: *the most formidable battles are not those we wage against the world but those that rage within us.* The brilliance of this often-overlooked chapter alerts us to the fact that to truly conquer the outer world, we must first master the world within.

> *"The most accurate test of valor is not the conquest of external foes but the appeasement of self-inflicted inner turmoil."*

As we complete the inaugural chapter of the Bhagavad Gita, it is essential to spotlight the traditional conclusion of every chapter within this timeless scripture. Each chapter culminates with a refrain reiterating its essence, serving as a thematic anchor and bridge to the subsequent teachings. While some scholars mention that these summary *shlokas* may have been introduced later by revered Acharyas of the teaching tradition, they do form an integral part of the Bhagavad Gita as it is read, studied, and taught today. These *shlokas* not only crystallize the teachings of each chapter but also weave the awe-inspiring history of Arjuna and Krishna into the expansive tapestry of the Vedic vision.

Concluding Cadence: Gita's Ethereal Essence

The first chapter concludes with:

|| ॐ तत्सदिति श्रीमद्भगवद्गीतासु उपनिषत्सु ब्रह्मविद्यायां योगशास्त्रे
श्रीकृष्णार्जुनसंवादे अर्जुनविषादयोगो नाम प्रथमोऽध्यायः ||

|| *ōṁ tatsaditi śrīmadbhagavadgītāsu upaniṣatsu*
brahmavidyāyāṁ yōgaśāstrē
śrīkṛṣṇārjunasaṁvādē arjunaviṣādayōgō nāma prathamō›dhyāyaḥ ||

Translation:

"Om, Brahman, is the only reality. Thus ends the first chapter called Arjuna Vishada Yoga – having the topic of Arjuna's sorrow – in the Bhagavad Gita, which is in the form of a dialogue between Shri Krishna and Arjuna, which is the essence of the Upanishads, whose subject matter is both the knowledge of Brahman and yoga."

Commentary:

The concluding verse of every chapter within the Bhagavad Gita reiterates, as it were, the essence of its content. It serves as a summary of what was said and a prelude to what will follow.

The *shloka* commences with the timeless invocation: *OM*, a sound representing the Absolute Reality of the universe—*Brahman*. As elucidated in Vedic literature, *Brahman* is the foundational reality of everything, including the universe. *Tat Sad* emphasizes that only one immutable and singular reality, *Brahman*, exists and is represented by the primal sound, *OM*.

The word *Srimad* honours the Bhagavad Gita as a treasure trove of wisdom. *Shri* symbolizes wealth in its multifaceted glory, encompassing knowledge (*Vidya*) that bestows upon us immeasurable riches. It is fitting that the Gita, with *Bhagavan* as the supreme teacher, is adorned with this title. As understood earlier, *Bhagavan* possesses absolute virtues, the six-fold *bhaga*: knowledge, power, wealth, fame, beauty, and dispassion. Indeed, the one befitting the title *Shriman* is *Bhagavan* alone.

The Bhagavad Gita is likened to the Upanishads in its vision and depth. Both serve as guiding lights that dispel the darkness of *samsara*, the cause of suffering in life. By equating the Gita to the Upanishads, we are reminded that the essence of both scriptures is *Brahma vidya—the* knowledge of *Brahman*, the Absolute Reality of the universe. The Bhagavad Gita is not merely a handbook of solace for the weary-hearted; it is a profound exploration of the nature of *Brahman*.

While *Brahma vidya* provides knowledge of this ultimate reality, the Path of Yoga offers practical means to attain spiritual maturity. In the context of the Gita, the *Yoga Shastra* covers various dimensions, from purifying the mind through *Karma* Yoga to achieving tranquility via *Upasana* Yoga and gaining understanding through *Jnana* Yoga. The Gita is thus a compendium of both profound wisdom and actionable knowledge.

The entire Bhagavad Gita is a dialogue between Krishna and the warrior prince, Arjuna. The profundity of the exchange reveals that their conversation is not just limited to the context of the battlefield of Kurukshetra but resonates with the inner tumult each of us faces.

The first chapter, aptly titled 'The Yoga of Arjuna's Sorrow,' does not advocate sorrow as a virtue but hails it as a starting point. Arjuna's despair is emblematic of the universal human struggle. It is a catalyst that can culminate in either introspection or escapism. Fortunately, under Krishna's sagacious guidance, Arjuna's sorrow becomes a gateway to deep contemplation and consequent realization of *Dharma*. Through Arjuna's dilemma we get a peek into the inner struggles and setbacks that we actively avoid all through our lives. Witnessing his vulnerabilities about to be addressed by Krishna, we are somehow able to gather hope to overcome our own plight.

These concluding *shlokas*, found at the end of each chapter of the Bhagavad Gita, emphatically reiterate the central theme of the chapter they are summing up. This *shloka* is a bridge, leading us from Arjuna's visceral sorrow to the profound wisdom that follows in subsequent chapters.

Summary of Arjuna Vishada Yoga

The first chapter, *Arjuna Vishada Yoga,* is a dramatic introduction to the Bhagavad Gita. It explores a pivotal moment on the battlefield of Kurukshetra. As the conch shells blare and the armies are poised for battle, we meet Arjuna, the pinnacle of virtue and valor. He stands, poised upon his chariot, between the two great forces, ready to embark on a righteous war. Yet, as he surveys the faces across the field, emotions around kinship and impending destruction begin to gnaw at his resolve. Familial ties clash with duty, and Arjuna is left intellectually, emotionally, and physically paralyzed. More than a tale of a warrior's faltering courage, this introductory chapter is an exposition of the collapse of the human personality when faced with a choice between what needs to be done and what one likes or does not like to do.

The Mahabharata battle can be analogized to the eternal struggle within the confines of our mind. On this internal battleground, *dharmic* (righteous) thoughts and *adharmic* (unrighteous) emotions constantly vie for dominance, shaping our decisions and, by extension, our destinies. Arjuna, in this context, represents the essence of self-control. He embodies the spirit that we require to manage life's myriad challenges. Every moment we grapple with choices, where righteousness is pitted against more accessible paths of transgression and the echoes of our inner Arjuna yearn for guidance, we are reminded of this ancient tale again.

In typical understanding, *vishada* (despondency) is deemed a weakness, an ailment that saps vitality. Yet, in the presence of Krishna, Arjuna's profound despair transforms, serving as the catalyst for one of the world's most enlightening spiritual discourses. The shift is histrionic: from *roga* (disease) to *yoga* (control and spiritual union). It underscores the transformative power of guidance. With the right mentor or guide, even our deepest sorrows can be channeled into paths of growth and enlightenment. Arjuna was fortunate to find his advice in none other than *Yogeshwara Bhagavan* Shri Krishna. Arjuna's crumbling initiates the sacred dialogue between the two, therefore serving as a necessary precursor to his transformation.

Arjuna Vishada Yoga mirrors the universality of human experiences. The dilemmas faced by Arjuna on the battlefield are very similar to the ones we encounter in our daily lives. While the setting may be ancient, the embedded lessons are timeless. They urge us to recognize our internal battles and, with introspection and wisdom, chalk out a path for ourselves that will lead us toward righteousness and Self-Realization.

To further elucidate the intricate layers of *Arjuna Vishada Yoga*, the table below provides a succinct enumeration of the chapter's shlokas and their implication in the Mahabharata and subjective context.

Shloka(s)

Context of the Mahabharata

Context of Battle within

1
Dhritarashtra's question to Sanjaya about the battlefield events
Curiosity of the blind mind to discern inner struggles

2
Duryodhana approaches his mentor, Drona.
The cautionary note: habits can dictate our decisions.

3-6
Listing the mighty heroes in Pandava's army
Recognizing the *Dharmic* forces in the mind

7-9
Listing the great warriors in the Kaurava ranks
Recognizing the *Adharmic* tendencies within

10-11

Kauravas strategize, emphasizing Bhishma's protection.
Adharmic forces rally to shield the ego, our deceptive self.

12-13

Bhishma leads the Kauravas, signaling with his conch.
The initial surge from ego and *Adharmic* instincts

14-19

The divine charioteer, Krishna, the warrior prince Arjuna, and the Pandava army respond with their conchs.
Response from the *Dharmic* thoughts and emotions, asserting purity

20-23

Arjuna requests to view the adversaries.
Self-control habitually gravitates toward inner *Adharmic* tendencies.

24-27

Arjuna observes the vast Kaurava assembly.
Self-control confronts the multitude of internal *adharmic* forces, leading to confusion.

28-31

Arjuna manifests signs of emotional distress.
Outward signs when one grapples with overwhelming inner turmoil

32-37

Arjuna's firm refusal to engage in battle
Self-mastery's reluctance to confront and combat destructive emotions and adverse thoughts

38-39

Arjuna's rationale behind his decision
Self-control's justification: all emotions, even the negative ones, are integral to our psychic nature.

40-44
Arjuna lists the disasters of a civil war.
Self-control appraises the hazards of waging an internal psychological battle.

45-46
Arjuna's inclination to withdraw from the conflict
The human propensity to yield to overwhelming emotions and desires

47
Arjuna's emotional paralysis
The moment when self-control feels utterly defenseless

Arjuna Vishada Yoga: *Shlokas* to Ponder

In its all-encompassing wisdom, the Bhagavad Gita offers lessons for the personality to learn and evolve from and deep contemplation for the mind to find equilibrium amidst life's clutter. It behooves us to hold close to a few critical *shlokas from* each chapter. Synchronizing fully with their in-depth meaning and reciting them in quiet introspection, moments of elation or despair will beget us guidance and solace right through our spiritual journey.

Let us look at some of the impactful *shlokas* from Chapter 1:

1: From Action to Purposeful Living

Dharmakṣētrē kurukṣētrē samavētā yuyutsavaḥ |
māmakāḥ pāṇḍavāścaiva kimakurvata sañjaya ||*1*||

The very first *shloka* of the Gita serves a great purpose in one's evolutionary journey as it highlights one's willingness to observe one's own life. To progress spiritually, one must be willing to reflect on and question the nature of one's actions. The distinction between merely engaging in life's activities (*Kurukshetra)* and leading a life of purpose and righteousness (*Dharma Kshetra*) is vividly highlighted here. By chanting this verse and mindfully observing our actions, we transition from mere activity to purposeful action.

2: A Symphony of Guidance

tataḥ śvētairhayairyuktē mahati syandanē sthitau |
mādhavaḥ pāṇḍavaścaiva divyau śaṅkhau pradadhmatuḥ ||14||

Krishna and Arjuna's dramatic introduction in this verse glorifies the harmonious coexistence of divine wisdom and human endeavor. This *shloka* is an ode to the interplay between spiritual guidance (represented by Krishna) and our conscious efforts (represented by Arjuna). Contemplating this verse can dispel mental distress and provide a sense of direction, emphasizing the importance of harmonizing our actions with spiritual wisdom.

3: The Weight of Overwhelm

ēvamuktvā›rjunaḥ saṅkhyē rathōpastha upāviśat |
visṛjya saśaraṁ cāpaṁ śōkasaṁvignamānasaḥ ||47||

This verse vividly animates Arjuna's despondency. It is a moment many can relate to—feeling overwhelmed and trapped by circumstances. However, we are powerfully reminded that even in our most challenging moments, when we surrender our burdens to a higher power or seek guidance from our inner Krishna, we can find a way out of despair.

These beautiful *shlokas* remind us that through the highs and lows of life, the wisdom of the Gita can be our guiding star, helping us navigate challenges and emerge stronger, wiser, and more attuned to our spiritual essence.

The Profound Purpose of Arjuna Vishada Yoga

Many approach the first chapter of the Bhagavad Gita with a million apprehensions. They wonder about its purpose as it does not abound with spiritual teachings, and Krishna speaks but half a *shloka* in between the 47 that are dedicated to Arjuna crying out his woes. The entire chapter is deeply entrenched in the complex storyline of the Mahabharata and lingers upon Arjuna's internal struggles amid a looming war. Modern Gita mentors sometimes even skip this chapter, deeming it superfluous. So, it begs the question: What is this chapter's true intent?

Beyond being a timeless spiritual scripture, the Bhagavad Gita is an enlightening treatise addressing the timeless human quandary. The great poet and sage Vyasa could have presented this problem abstractly, yet he brilliantly weaves it into a historical context. Chapter one is not inconsistent with the enlightening wisdom from the mouth of Shri Krishna that is to follow. When exhaustively understood, it unravels as a meticulous exposition of universal human sufferings and a stimulus that elicits eternal wisdom.

Imagine living a life where efficiency, consistency, and effectiveness effortlessly align. Most of us strive for such an existence, yet these ideals often teeter based on our circumstances. Our spirits soar when things align with our desires and everything feels well within our control. Yet, when life throws a curveball, we falter, feeling perplexed and overwhelmed.

The ancient teachings of *Vedanta* illuminate this phenomenon, attributing our emotional fluctuations to *Raga* (binding attachments) and *Dvesha* (aversions). Picture yourself fervently craving a promotion at work. If an equally deserving colleague secures it instead, it challenges your *Raga*, and turmoil ensues. Similarly, if you have always detested public speaking and are suddenly thrust into giving a presentation, it challenges your *Dvesha*, and the emotional upheaval can be immense. Such impediments cloud judgment, often leading us to act against our better wisdom or, like Arjuna, leaving us paralyzed in indecision.

The promise of the Bhagavad Gita is transformative. It aspires to rise above and commandeer any situation by helping us align our worldly and spiritual pursuits. As the great master Shankara insightfully observes in his introduction to the Gita, *it holds the potential to foster economic and social welfare while catalyzing spiritual ascension.*

By presenting Arjuna's profound despair, a challenge exponentially more daunting than most of us will ever face, the Gita subtly reminds us of its universal applicability. If Arjuna, standing at the precipice of a civil war, can find clarity and purpose through the teachings of the Bhagavad Gita, then indeed, in the throes of our relatively more uncomplicated challenges, so can we. It reminds us that every darkness experienced is an opportunity to go inward and turn on our inner light. This is the essence of *Vishada Yoga.*

While the context presented here is a historical battlefield strewn with eclectic characters from a particular era, the highlighted human challenges remain perennial. Arjuna's dilemmas are thus universally relatable, thereby rendering the timeless message of the Bhagavad Gita relevant across epochs and cultures. Arjuna's predicament, though confronted and conquered in the past, continues to resonate in our contemporary struggles. The Bhagavad Gita, thus, continues to be hailed as a historical scripture and a living testament to human resilience and spiritual evolution.

"Life is our Kurukshetra, and within us lies an Arjuna, yearning for wisdom to navigate life's challenges."

Life Lessons from Arjuna Vishada Yoga

Many truths and life lessons have emerged from our study of Arjuna Vishada Yoga. Beyond being a poetic portrayal of a warrior's dilemma, this chapter has helped us identify our daily internal struggles.

The Bhagavad Gita is not meant for reverence or philosophical musings alone. It is a handbook for life. Extracted from this divine dialogue between a sincere seeker and his Spiritual teacher are pearls of wisdom that stand out for their depth and immense practical applicability. Here are some of the most significant takeaways:

The Power of Introspection: Reflecting upon our actions, emotions, and decisions is invaluable. Through such introspective journeys, we discern patterns, understand our inherent nature, and strive for improvement.

Beware the Mind's Persuasion: Very tactfully, the mind nudges us into justifying improper thoughts and makes us helplessly succumb to momentary emotions and harmful temptations. It is crucial to recognize and navigate these mental mazes.

Rebellion Isn't Always the Answer: Faced with challenges or needing discipline, an impulsive or rebellious reaction is never the best choice. It is always more prudent to respond with balance and poise.

Mastery Over Suppression: Through an overwhelming surge, simply suppressing emotions is not the solution. A more sustainable approach is to strive for understanding and self-mastery through various yoga practices elucidated within the Bhagavad Gita.

nurtured over time. Recognizing and actively working to overcome detrimental habits is critical to personal growth.

Decision-making in Calm Waters: Avoid making pivotal decisions when the mind is overwhelmed or disturbed. Sound judgments and wise choices rarely spring from a tumultuous or weak mindset.

Adherence to *Dharma*: Amidst life's myriad challenges and moral dilemmas, adhering to *Dharma*—righteousness and duty—should be paramount. Even when faced with conflicts, prioritizing what should be done, as *Dharma* dictates, can be life's most significant investment.

The Need for Spiritual Wisdom: Tapping into the spiritual reservoir within or discovering our inner Krishna can be supremely transformative. Regular spiritual practices like prayer, studying sacred scriptures, and aligning with *Dharmic* principles are essential to keeping this connection with the Divine alive and active.

Arjuna Vishada Yoga beckons us to delve into the symbolic depth of the drama at play, unearth the wisdom buried within each scene, and embark upon a transformative journey guided by introspection and self-discipline.

Closing Remarks

An in-depth exploration of the first chapter and Arjuna's distress, in particular, mirrors typical human predicaments. It begins to introduce us to ways that will help us rise above them.

This universally resonant tale of an ancient warrior's inner struggle reminds us of our daily confrontations within. Yet, as insightful as it is, this opening merely sets the stage. In the subsequent volume of this series, we will present a detailed analysis of the second chapter that unveils *Bhagavan* Shri Krishna's transformative teachings. When we take up the study of the *shlokas* in the second chapter, we will understand the indispensable necessity and true purpose of the first.

Reflections and Aspirations

From Lessons Learned to the Vision Ahead

"As the rays of the sun dispel darkness, so does the wisdom of the Bhagavad Gita dispel ignorance. We pledge to spread its luminance to every corner of our world."

Reflecting on the Journey

As we rewind the clock to the inception of this endeavor, we are awash with reverence, humility, and joy. Together, we embarked on this sacred expedition not just as co-authors wishing to "enlighten" the world with fresh insights into this ancient knowledge but as earnest seekers yearning to crystallize our own understandings even further.

Yogi Bhajan puts it so beautifully: "If you want to learn something, read about it. If you want to understand something, write about it. If you want to master something, teach it."

Our earnest sharing of this knowledge is but a deepening of our own *sadhana* in the hope that it will help transform the lives of as many as it encounters the way it is transforming ours.

With this being our first offering in 'The Gita Odyssey' series, we hope our unique threefold perspective has sparked your interest in delving deeper into the spiritual wisdom of the Bhagavad Gita.

Heartfelt Harmonies: The Trio Behind the Odyssey

Three distinct notes found each other across international borders despite the disparity between their life journeys and came together to create a new and vibrant symphony of this ancient wisdom cherished as the Bhagavad Gita. Rajesh Rabindranath, Vikrant Singh Tomar, and Avanti Kundalia, from the United States, India, and Singapore, respectively, were magnetized as kindred spirits united by a profound reverence for the teachings of the Gita. Each, having independently studied, applied, and taught the Bhagavad Gita for years before they met, discovered a shared luminosity in their interpretations and articulations. Their synergy was miraculous; often, one voice seamlessly continued where another left off.

The bond between Rajesh and Vikrant dates back to 2013—a spiritual brotherhood that transcends conventional relationships and is strengthened by shared insights and spiritual revelations. When Avanti joined their ranks in 2023, she seamlessly integrated with this duo, resonating with the same spiritual frequency. Their collective vision for the propagation of the Bhagavad Gita and their shared camaraderie, infused with mutual respect and unconditional love, echo as the heartbeat of this book.

Heartfelt Notes from the Author Trio

Namaste, Divine Companions,

In every life, there is a calling that resonates with our very essence—a mission we eagerly pursue as our tribute to the universe. For me, that mission is heartfelt and straightforward: to make the Gita's transformative teachings accessible to all earnest seekers. My journey with this sacred text began unexpectedly during my college years, a path I now see was likely shaped by the undercurrents of past *karma*. Initially puzzling, the Gita drew me in with its promise of deep insight. My path to understanding was first illuminated by the teachings of Swami Chinmayananda, whose wisdom reached me despite our paths having never crossed directly. Yet, it was under Swami Dayananda Saraswati's direct guidance that I acquired the ability to unravel the Gita's profound verses—a skill that breathed life into its teachings for me. This deep connection with the Gita has solidified my belief in its life-changing power. This insight has inspired me to initiate Project Self, where we facilitate sessions sharing this ancient wisdom. 'The Divine Canvas' is not just a project; it is the manifestation of a lifelong dream and vision, now unfolding with grace. As we release the first book in this endeavor, I am filled with a profound sense of blessing and fulfillment.

In this moment of reflection, my heart fills with immense gratitude toward the Divine for guiding me in this sacred endeavor. I offer my profound reverence to Lord Shiva, the *Adi guru*, and to Sai Baba of Shirdi, whose grace has been a pillar of my strength. With deep respect, I honor the teaching lineage of the Bhagavad Gita—*Bhagavan* Shri Krishna, Sage Vyasa, and Adi Shankaracharya, whose timeless teachings echo through the ages. I am eternally indebted to Sri Narayana Guru, whose influence on my life is beyond words. My sincere appreciation extends to Swami Sarvapriyananda and Acharya Vivek Gupta for their personal guidance and unyielding support. I offer my love and respect to Swami Shantananda and Swami Tadatmananda for their insightful classes on the Gita that have enriched my journey.

I am forever grateful to my parents and my sister, Renjini, whose nurturing has shaped my path, and to my uncle, the late P.N. Narendranathan Nair, for introducing me to the realms of spirituality. I acknowledge my cousin Maya and my uncle Santhosh for enriching my childhood with everlasting memories.

A special note of thanks to my academic mentors, Mr. C.K. Venkatesh and R. Parthiban, whose influence permeates my approach to learning and teaching. To friends like Sunil Veettil and Sajeev Kumar, your unwavering support has been my stronghold. To my colleagues and mentors—Mr. Bill Perkins, Sarji Mohammedali, Ilio Krumins-Beens,

Don Pollitt, Linda Broderick, and Ginny Aiden—thank you for your mentorship and support. The Project Self Team, my second family, turns my dreams into realities with unwavering dedication—your collective efforts are the backbone of this vision. To K.I. Alexander, thank you for your friendship and the soul-stirring music that invariably brightens my days. Finally, to each member of the Gita Insight Squad and Gita Deep Learning Members, your engagement is what has brought this dream to its full and vibrant life.

I extend a warm embrace to my co-author, Avanti Kundalia, guide Bhuvana Iyer, and my dear friends Sanjay Rajput, Venkat Sriramalu, Karthik Palamalai, Prasad Akavoor, Rajesh Menon, and Jeena Suresh, who ignited the spark for this book. My apologies to anyone I may have inadvertently missed—know that your support has not gone unnoticed.

Lastly, to the loves of my life—Deepthy, Daksha, Vikrant, and Avneet—your love and presence give meaning to my every day. At the core of my universe is my wife, Deepthy; her arrival in my life has made it meaningful. To her, I lovingly dedicate the first book in this series. Our daughter Daksha's presence fills my heart with love and joy, a shining testament to life's blessings. Vikrant Singh Tomar and Avneet Baid, my spiritual siblings, have graced my journey with a bond that transcends the mere ties of tradition, enriching my life with their unconditional support and camaraderie. Together, you are my sanctuary, inspiration, and family beyond blood.

In closing, this book is as much yours as it is mine, for your companionship on this journey has made all this possible. May the wisdom of the Gita touch your lives as it has profoundly touched mine.

Blessings and gratitude,
Rajesh Rabindranath

सदाशिव समारम्भाम् शंकराचार्य मध्यमाम्
अस्मद् आचार्य पर्यन्ताम् वंदे गुरु परम्पराम्...

Namaste,

I pay homage to the sacred land of Bharat, where the wisdom of great saints and sages, the custodians of Vedic mantras, found its expression. I remain forever indebted to luminaries such as Maharshi Vedavyasa, Maharshi Patanjali, Adi Shankaracharya, Swami Ramakrishna Paramahansa, Swami Vivekananda, Swami Chinmayananda, Swami Dayananda, Dr. Sarvepalli Radhakrishnan, Swami Paramarthananda, Swami Ranganathananda, and all those Masters whose writings, thoughts, and contributions serve as a wellspring for my comprehension of the scriptures.

I offer my deepest gratitude to Shweta, Shourya, and Titiksha for their unwavering support. I extend my appreciation to Dr. Vikrant Shah for his stimulating and thought-provoking discussions, which were instrumental in nurturing my creative thinking throughout the writing process of this book. I am sincerely grateful to Shri Rajesh Rabindranath for his unwavering dedication to providing clarity, scriptural precision, traditional authenticity, and a well-structured framework for this book. Furthermore, I extend my heartfelt appreciation to Mrs. Avanti Kundalia for her invaluable contribution in articulating the most appropriate words and meanings for the timeless and divine message of the Bhagavad Gita.

I dedicate this book to my beloved mother, Mrs. Saroj Tomar, whose unconditional love and blessings continue to play a pivotal role in all my undertakings.

I humbly bow before all the known and unknown divine forces that have facilitated our journey in bringing this work to fruition.

With you in Consciousness,
Dr. Vikrant Singh Tomar
Namaskaar!

The Divine in me truly bows with utmost humility to the Divine in you.

The first chapter of the Bhagavad Gita is titled *Arjuna Vishada Yoga*, which translates as "The Yoga of Arjuna's Grief." Grief, as taught in the Gita, can be one's most significant catalyst for dramatic spiritual edification. And so, it was for me.

The loss of my mother at the tender age of seven had me pacing the alleys of every spiritual sanctuary, seeking the answer to the simple question, "Why me?" My quest began in a church in Panchgani, Maharashtra, India, where I went to boarding school from age five to 15. It was fortified by my ajji (maternal grandmother), Late Smt. Rajkamal Redij, and maushi (maternal aunt), Smt. Reema Rajeev, both devoutly committed to the ritualistic traditions of *Sanatan Dharma*. It found its fulfillment in the study of Vedanta, which soon became my full-time pursuit.

I could not shake the belief that there must be more to life than meets the eye. This curiosity earned me distinctions in various esoteric modalities: Diploma in Teaching Hatha Yoga and Meditation from Gita International Yoga Institute, Melbourne, Australia Certificate in Life Coaching from Soul Center, Singapore Reiki Master from the Reiki Center, Singapore, among others.

I had the good fortune of studying and serving at Chinmaya Mission for more than two decades under the tutelage of Swami Swaroopananda (the Global Head of Chinmaya Mission), who initiated me into Scriptural studies. Life blessed me with a tremendous guide in MitrananadaJi (Spiritual Mentor Chinmaya Mission Chennai and Northeast Bharat), who roused me to translate my innate talents, core passions, and bottomless love for *Bharat* and *Sanatan Dharma* into dynamic service to society. Finally, a life-transforming three-year Vedanta course with A. ParthasarathyJi (Vedanta Academy, Malavali, India) awarded me with my life's vision and mission to spread the knowledge of Advaita Vedanta as far and wide as I could.

By a miraculous twist of fate, I was introduced to Project Self while keenly looking to partner with a non-religious institution in the service of the evolution of human consciousness. Dr. Vikrant Singh Tomar, Sanjay Rajput, and Rajesh Rabindranath of Project Self stepped into my life in quick succession for the realization of this never-thought-of possibility of co-authoring a commentary on the Bhagavad Gita. In record time. Their steady companionship through this enlightening journey, coupled with the ever-welcoming embrace of the core team members of Project Self and United Consciousness, has been invaluable.

The Bhagavad Gita has been a constant source of wisdom, strength, and solace in my life. Her infallible guidance, in more ways than one, replaced the biological mother I never fully experienced. The Gita has comforted me through every tear, cheerfully rallied around my every smile, and sternly guided my every step. Ours truly is a connection that I have felt with nothing or no one through this mortal journey of mine.

My unique understanding and articulation of her teachings have transformed my life and the lives of my students in miraculous ways. I am blessed to express my gratitude for life's perfect unfolding under her sheltering umbrella by sharing some of those transformative insights through this book.

As Mark Twain says, "The two most important days in your life are the day you were born and the day you find out why." I humbly bow before the unfathomable grace of Providence (loosely called "God") for both!

This enormous initiative would have been impossible without the love and support of my Baba, Dr. Dilip Borawake, my sisters Smt. Kaveri Mulay and Reva, my husband Biren, and my beloved children Pooja and Krishna. I raise this book to the sky for my father-in-law, the late Dr. Harish Kundalia, my greatest cheerleader, who would have been so proud of me.

Above all, I dedicate this labor of love to my earnest students, who continue to place their unwavering faith in my sharing of this Vedantic knowledge with them. The transformations I witnessed in their lives through the Bhagavad Gita classes are what ignited my dormant will to put this knowledge out in as many ways as possible. Their ever-constant encouragement infused me with the courage to actually do so.

Nimmita Maatram: But an Instument...
Avanti Kundalia

The Road Ahead: Charting the Gita Odyssey

Any spiritual quest draws seekers into the uncharted depths of their inner world. As you, dear reader, turned the pages of this foundational tome, you were not merely being exposed to fresh new perspectives on age-old wisdom; you were being introduced to new facets of Self-discovery. This is only the first step. It will be our honor to walk alongside you through the rest of the Gita Odyssey.

The Gita Odyssey aspires to span 18 books, each uniquely designed to be an exciting milestone for readers to reach during their study of the Bhagavad Gita.

In our heartfelt endeavor to make the wisdom of the Gita accessible to diverse readers across regions, we have undertaken an initiative beyond just translations. We are re-envisioning its essence, tailored to the unique cadence of various languages. These will not just be linguistic adaptations, but comprehensive reinterpretations designed to resonate deeply with each audience's cultural and linguistic nuance.

Through the Gita Odyssey, we hope to provide a clear and structured path for any seeker desiring to delve into the depths of the Bhagavad Gita. We anticipate that with each book, your understanding of the subject matter will broaden and thereby deepen your connection with its teachings.

Unveiling the Divine Canvas Project

We are pleased to reveal that this book is but the first installment of an expansive vision conceived and nurtured by Project Self, a dedicated nonprofit organization based in New Jersey, USA.

Welcome to the Divine Canvas Project, where the Bhagavad Gita is studied and shared on an unparalleled scale for the contemporary seeker.

The Vision Behind Divine Canvas

The Divine Canvas project has been designed to unravel the profound wisdom embedded within the sacred *shlokas of* the Bhagavad Gita. Its objective is to create an all-encompassing knowledge base on the Gita, all while ensuring its teachings remain relevant and applicable in today's fast-paced world.

Firmly rooted in the Advaita Vedanta tradition, this initiative offers insights that foster a profound understanding of the Gita's vision. It seamlessly bridges the chasm between ancient wisdom and modern perspectives, ensuring that the Gita's timeless teachings resonate with a diverse audience across the globe.

The Divine Canvas is all-inclusive, breaking down barriers of caste, creed, religion, nationality, and even educational or professional status. Everyone from every corner of the world is invited. It is not about where you come from but where you wish to go in your quest for knowledge and personal growth that matters.

The Pillars of Our Mission

Unveiling Profound Wisdom: Researching and aligning perspectives from insightful commentaries of all prominent masters hailing from the Advaita Vedanta tradition, the project aims to create a vast knowledge base of the Bhagavad Gita under one umbrella.

Harnessing AI: Leveraging the power and potential of artificial intelligence, the team envisions a module that offers personalized guidance, ensuring every seeker finds their unique path in understanding Gita's teachings.

Literary Endeavors: By releasing a series of 18 books and numerous supplementary volumes, the teachings of the Gita will find a new voice accessible in multiple languages.

Embracing Modern Tools: An AI-powered Learning Management System is in the making, promising tailored learning experiences across various languages.

Art and Inspiration: The project is not confined to words alone. From 21 soul-stirring songs that capture the essence of each chapter, a play animating its wisdom, inspiring paintings, to Gita chanting records, every artistic avenue is being explored to disseminate in the most creative ways the knowledge of the Gita.

Fostering a Community: Efforts are underway to groom teachers and conduct multilingual live classes, fostering an environment of interactive discussions and exploration exclusively dedicated to propagating the wisdom of the Gita across the globe.

Your Invitation to a Timeless Exploration

The Divine Canvas project is a comprehensive platform designed for those yearning for transformative experiences through the study of the Bhagavad Gita. Every endeavor, from art to technology, reaffirms our commitment to authenticity and the mission of self-discovery.

Standing at the dawn of a new age of global enlightenment, we warmly invite you to journey with us. Join hands with the Divine Canvas project, an initiative where the radiant teachings of the Bhagavad Gita are waiting to illuminate countless lives, including yours. Together, may we create a future where ancient wisdom becomes the guiding light for all.

Project Self: The Heartbeat Behind the Mission

Founded on the auspicious Vijaya Dashami day of 2014 by a dedicated group of 12 professionals, Project Self has since been a source of unwavering support and assistance for those pursuing holistic well-being. As a nonprofit organization based in New Jersey, USA, its mission transcends conventional boundaries, aiming to empower individuals in every facet of their lives. Combining age-old wisdom with modern practices, the organization curates many activities that address the physical, psychological, intellectual, social, and spiritual well-being of the community. Whether it is the solace provided by yoga sessions, the calmness derived from our meditation classes, or the growth experienced through our skill enhancement workshops and spiritual programs, Project Self fosters an environment teeming with compassion, understanding, and spiritual wisdom.

The Divine Canvas Project is a testament to Project Self's unwavering dedication and commitment. Throughout the years, Project Self has passionately sought to shine a guiding light for seekers, creating a haven where acceptance and comprehension thrive. Their longstanding commitment to sharing the eternal wisdom of the Bhagavad Gita since 2014 empowers this dedication. Project Self invites you to join our nurturing community, where the pursuit of overall wellness is a collective dream. For a better understanding of our vision and offerings, visit https://pself.org.

Concluding Reflections

From the depths of our hearts, we thank you for journeying with us through the pages of this book. We earnestly urge you to complement your study with the myriad tools that go hand in hand with the Divine Canvas project, be it our e-learning platform, the intuitive mobile app, or engaging live classes. The profound wisdom of the Bhagavad is a transformative elixir that, when taken with devotion, can bring about a paradigm shift potent enough to reshape the scripts of our lives.

As seekers, we are blessed with masterful commentaries written by some of the most luminous intellects the world has ever seen. And so, we cannot deny that our minds doubted and our hands trembled in daring to write one ourselves. But knowledge sincerely shared is knowledge gained.

We collectively pledge our unwavering commitment to continually document and share the wisdom we are blessed to uncover as we continue to apply the teachings of the Gita to our daily lives. Should our steps falter or there be any inadvertent errors or oversights, we humbly seek your forgiveness, feedback, and guidance. We are all in this together—yearning, seeking, discovering, learning, imbibing, experimenting, and steadily evolving.

May the grace and blessings of *Bhagavan* Shri Krishna through His celestial song guide each of us to a life of material prosperity, inner peace, and ultimately, the realization of the Self.

References

1. Sustainable Development Solutions Network. (2021). World Happiness Report 2021.
2. Diener, E., & Seligman, M. E. P. (2002). Very happy people. Psychological Science, 13(1), 81-84
3. Olfson, M., Marcus, S. C., Druss, B., Elinson, L., Tanielian, T., & Pincus, H. A. (2002). National trends in the outpatient treatment of depression. JAMA, 287(2), 203-209.
4. American Psychological Association. (2022, January). Special report: Burnout and stress. Monitor on Psychology, 53(1)
5. Twenge, J. M., Campbell, W. K., & Martin, G. N. (2018). Decreases in psychological well-being among American adolescents after 2012 and links to screen time during the rise of smartphone technology. Emotion, 18(6), 765-780.
6. Schopenhauer, Arthur. Parerga and Paralipomena. Vol. 2. Translated by E.F.J. Payne. Oxford University Press, 1892. p. 120.
7. Seligman, M. E. P. (2002). Authentic Happiness: Using the New Positive Psychology to Realize Your Potential for Lasting Fulfillment. Free Press.
8. Saraswati, Swami Dayananda. Bhagavad Gita - Volume 1 (Bhagavad Gita Series (English)) (p. 42). Arsha Vidya Research and Publication Trust. Kindle Edition.
9. Chinmayananda, Swami. The Holy Geeta (p. 78). Central Chinmaya Mission Trust. Kindle Edition.

10. Saraswati, Swami Dayananda. Introduction to Vedanta. Vision Books Pvt. Ltd., New Delhi, India, 2014. ISBN 81-7094-289-6.
11. Aristotle. Nicomachean Ethics. Book VI, Chapter 8.
12. Davis, Richard. H. The Bhagavad Gita: A Biography. Princeton University Press, 2014.
13. Theosophy of the Bhagavad Gita. Blavatsky Theosophy. Accessed October 20, 2023. https://blavatskytheosophy.com/the-theosophy-of-the-bhagavad-gita/
14. Sundariyal, Shambhoo P. Influence of the Bhagavadgita on the poetry of W.B. Yeats
15. Divya Jyoti Jagrati Sansthan. "The Bhagavad Gita and the Indian Freedom Struggle." Divya Jyoti Jagrati Sansthan, 2018. https://www.djjs.org/blog/bhagavad-gita-and-the-indian-freedom-struggle. Accessed October 21, 2023
16. Gandhi, M.K. The Bhagavad Gita According to Gandhi. Translated by Mahadev Desai. Wilder Publications, 2012.
17. Huxley, A. (1945). The perennial philosophy. Harper & Brothers.
18. Hijiya, James A. (2000). "The "Gita" of J. Robert Oppenheimer" (PDF). Proceedings of the American Philosophical Society. 144 (2)
19. Steiner, Rudolf, The Bhagavad Gita and the West: The Esoteric Significance of the Bhagavad Gita and Its Relation to the Epistles of Paul, p. 43
20. The Huston Smith Reader. p. 122
21. Valpey, K. R. (2022). Ethics of oneness: Emerson, Whitman, and the Bhagavad Gita. University of Chicago Press.
22. George Anastaplo (2002). But Not Philosophy: Seven Introductions to Non-Western Thought. Lexington.
23. The Economist. (2006, November 9). Bulent Ecevit: A politician with a poet's soul. [Obituary]. Retrieved from https://www.economist.com/obituary/2006/11/09/bulent-ecevit

24. M. K. Gandhi, Gandhi's Autobiography: The Story of My Experiments with Truth. Translated from Gujarati by Mahadev Desai. 1948, Washington, D. C.: Public Affairs Press
25. Chinmayananda, Swami. (2021). The Holy Geeta. Chinmaya Mission Trust.
26. Ranganathananda, Swami. (2023). The Universal Message of the Bhagavad Gita: An Exposition. Bharatiya Vidya Bhavan.
27. Swami Abhedananda. (2023). The Gospel of Ramakrishna. Abhedananda Publishing House
28. Yogananda, Paramahamsa. (2021). God Talks with Arjuna: The Bhagavad Gita [Ebook]. Self-Realization Fellowship
29. Shakespeare, W. (2023). Hamlet [Ebook]. HarperCollins Publishers.
30. Nataraja Guru, S. (2022). The Bhagavad Gita: Sublime Dialectics. Orient Blackswan Private Limited
31. Urban Balance. (2023, July 25). The story of the two wolves. Retrieved from https://www.urbanbalance.com/the-story-of-two-wolves/
32. William Ernest Henley, "Invictus" (1875).

General References:

1. Saraswati, Swami Paramarthananda. Bhagavad Gita Lecture Series. Audio recording. Sastraparakashika Trust, 2002
2. Arsha Bodha Center. (2011). Gita 2011. Retrieved from https://arshabodha.org/teachings/gita-2011/
3. Arsha Bodha Center. (n.d.). Teachings. Retrieved from https://arshabodha.org/teachings/
4. Parthasarathy, R. (2023). The Bhagavad Gita [Ebook]. Penguin Books India.
5. Teachings of Swami Dayananda. (2023). [Mobile app]. Apple App Store. https://apps.apple.com/us/app/teachings-of-swami-dayananda/id807400667

www.ingramcontent.com/pod-product-compliance
Lightning Source LLC
LaVergne TN
LVHW041203150826
845673LV00001B/269
9798891867802